D0790752

For all you've poured out,
may God restore, refresh
renew!

monica Leak
#Girl Get Your Life 2019

#no more HASH tags

Remembrance and Reflections

Monica Leak

Library of Congress Control Number:		2018904112
ISBN:	Hardcover	978-1-9845-1857-6
	Softcover	978-1-9845-1858-3
	eBook	978-1-9845-1859-0

Every attempt has been made to cite the specific work and authors, and any oversight is welcome for correction so that proper attribution can be made in future publications.

Scripture quotations taken from the Matthew Henry Study Bible, King James Version Copyright, 1994, 1997 by Word Bible Publishers, Inc. Used by permission.

Scripture taken from the New King James Version. Copyright 1982 by Thomas Nelson. Used by permission. All rights reserved.

Lana M. Hooks and Jonathan Susehimi, Editors
Derek Robinson, Cover Design
Cara-Lynn Birts, Photographer

Print information available on the last page.

Rev. date: 05/17/2018

To order additional copies of this book, contact:
Xlibris
1-888-795-4274
www.Xlibris.com
Orders@Xlibris.com
776909

We dedicate this collection to
sisters and brothers,
those whose stories were made known
and those yet unknown.
We say your name. We remember. We reflect.
We call for a revival of the heart, mind, and spirit
that will unite us as a people
to do the work to bring liberty and justice for all.

ACKNOWLEDGMENTS
To God who graces us with creativity;
To my family who offered time and space to grow and just be;
To the fivefold ministry that nurtured
and encouraged the call;
To my village of sisters, brothers, colleagues, and
friends who have supported me through it all;
May the love, peace, and joy of God be with you
and his blessings overtake you.

CONTENTS

#SayHerName

"10 WHO CAN FIND A VIRTUOUS WOMAN? FOR HER PRICE IS FAR ABOVE RUBIES.
25 STRENGTH AND HONOUR ARE HER CLOTHING; AND SHE SHALL REJOICE IN TIME TO COME.
26 SHE OPENETH HER MOUTH WITH WISDOM; AND IN HER TONGUE IS THE LAW OF KINDNESS.
31 GIVE HER OF THE FRUIT OF HER HANDS; AND LET HER OWN WORKS PRAISE HER IN THE GATES."

PROVERBS 31:10, 25–26, 31 (KJV)

Prayer of Confession

I open my mouth 'cause I have something to say,
Got something to get off my chest.
Early morning declarations of the day,
Tired and weary in search of rest.
To my back, this burden binds,
Good for the soul,
For peace of mind,
For that which will make me whole.

Confession

So these words of confession who would repeat?
Lest it become gossip, but in truth is my testimony.
I confess gratitude for being born in daunting
shades of brown,
You know, the color that makes you clutch your
purse in the elevator,
The colors that make you dash to your car quickly
and hit that door lock sound.
I confess to using my full vocal volume and range,
Echoing demands, for justice and resistance,
creating my own movement for change.
Yeah, I know there are times for quiet, but right
now, I've just got to be loud,
'Cause the message has got to move the crowd.

Confession

I do confess that I am fearfully and wonderfully made in the divine image,
Folks getting lifts and injections rushing like a high school football scrimmage.
Lips, full and pouty, soft and smooth;
Hips, legs, and thighs rocking any style that fits my mood.
Dark piercing eyes ability to discern;
Mind full of wisdom from the ancestors learned.
With the strength of my hands, I hold and lift,
Arms extended to give service, embrace, and cause shifts.

Confession

Creative ideas and witty inventions constantly running through my head,
Manifested businesses, programs, and projects leaving a legacy long after I'm dead.
Ever learning, seeking knowledge of the truth,
I confess I ask the hard questions not just accepting the answer that comes from you.
Yes, I do read, do research and gather the facts;
I sort through all that is available to know before letting my gut react.
But I do confess that sometimes stuff gets real,
Watching brothers and sisters getting killed in the streets, how can one be silent or still?
My heart is heavy and my soul is grieved
For every family losing someone beloved to police brutality.

Confession

From the top of my head to the soles of my feet,
in God, I do believe,
Yet when these events snowball, I lift my hands
and say, where is He?
I open that good book, flipping through its
weathered pages,
Crying out like the words of the psalmists, "Why
do the heathen keep raging?"
Bed soaked with tears,
Struggling to keep my head held high amid night
terrors and fears.
So this is my confession,
Letters and calls to congressmen and senators,
Reminding them, "I may not have voted for you,
but it is me you're working for."
I make myself visible with every call, every email
or letter that I write,
Sitting in the capital lobby, begging, calling on
leaders to do what is right.
At rallies in solidarity to plead the common cause,
The cause of justice belongs to all humanity, not
just yours.

Confession

So here I have confessed with my mouth the
truth of who I am,
To acknowledge what I believe as much as I
possibly can.
I speak knowing that there is much that I have
yet to understand,
That the solution to these issues of race and
equality won't be solved by waving a hand.
As struggles and turmoil yet lie ahead,

We have the strength of our faith and conviction in the path are forebears led.
I believe that justice and my humanity are a God-given birthright,
To this end, we march, protest and to this end, we sacrifice.
Belief unto righteousness;
Confession unto salvation,
Until the hope of liberty and justice for all is realized.

Confession

You Betta Run

You betta run
You betta run
Sista in a disabled car with a gun

You betta run
You betta run
Done broke her window
While her friend for help had gone

You betta run
You betta run
'Cause on the car seat
Sista got a gun

You betta run
You betta run
                    Because the sista you couldn't rouse
          Reason enough to break the window and fire
                                    twenty-four rounds

You betta run
You betta run
On that sista's lap, she got a gun

                              Wouldn't you be scared too
                                          Service station
                                         Vehicle stranded
                                        Locked in all alone
                                          Shots were fired
                              Before you got the sista's gun
                        Saying there's insufficient evidence

Policemen yet fired
Before completing an attempt to disarm
Just acting out of fear

Yeah, you betta run
You betta run and check that Bill of Rights
'Cause a sista citizen has a right to have a gun
Policies and practices are going to be checked
No criminal charges, but for the family just a
little settlement

The final outcome
The community cries
While the death of another black woman is
justified

Yeah, you betta run

#ForTyishaMiller

Monica Leak

They Be Comin'

They be comin' round the corner
They be comin' down the street
They be riding on cycles and bikes
Even when they're off their beat
When they come . . .
They be comin' late at night
They be comin' to pull over your car
Don't matter if it's a rental
Just don't plan on gettin' far

They be comin' single siren
They be comin' with lights of blue
They be comin' shining flashlights
Sayin' they recognize you
When they come . . .
They be comin' calling for backup
They be comin' to pull you out
They be comin' to grab you by your hair
What the bleep is that all about
When they come . . .

They be comin' with the pepper spray
They be comin' with a taser
They be comin' to put a gun to your head
Cop felt like he was falling back, as said to the paper
When they come . . .
Fired one bullet
One bullet struck the hip
Traveled to the lower rib cage
Death took its grip
When they come . . .

A warrant for a non-court appearance couldn't be served during the day?
So let's get a big cop to serve the warrant late at night on the freeway.
Yeah, that's the way they be comin'.
Comin' arousing fear and anxiety
Comin' not knowing if it's the last you'll be seen

Comin' going out to eat after a murder
Yet only the victim gets vilified
Cops only suspended
Motherless child, community unmended
When they come.

#ForKendraJames

Oops, My Bad

It takes a certain type
Problem-solving type
Good-judgment type
Multitasking type
Responsible type
Resourceful type
Assertive type
Collaborative type
Engaging type
Resourceful type
Empathetic type
Courageous type
One of integrity type
The type to enforce the law
The type that engages the community
The type that knows the community
Yeah, you know the type
No-knock-search-warrant type
Early-morning-break-down-door type
Woman-dressed-for-work-yet-handcuffed type
Battering-ram type
Grenade-throwing type
Explosion type
Oops, my bad
No armed people
Oops, my bad
No dogs
Oops, my bad
Just a city-government-employee type
Oops, my bad
6:10 a.m. raid

Oops, my bad
Oh no, wrong-apartment-layout type
Oops, my bad
Trusted-the-word-of-a-drug-dealer-trying-to-
save-his-
hide type
Oops, my bad
Heart condition
Ambulance requested
En route, cardiac arrested
7:50 a.m. dead

Oops, my bad

Tragic
Terrible episode
Slipshod police work
I'm-sorry type
These-things-happen type

Oops, my bad

Confidential informant
No prior surveillance conducted
Officers not from the precinct, what?
Warrant signed by a judging type
Now you want to question informant credibility

Oops, my bad

Condolences-and-sympathy-offered type
Should not have happened
Should not have happened
Hardworking type
Churchgoing type
Minded-her-business type
Talked-to-her-neighbors type

Should not have happened
Should not have happened
Should not have happened
Should not have happened
Should not have happened

#ForAlbertaSpruill

Ms. Johnston

Don't nobody betta come for Ms. Johnston.
Don't nobody betta come for Ms. Johnston.

A ninety-two-year-old woman living alone,
Wasn't expecting a gang of police officers to bust into her home.
Expecting to arrest a man for illegal drugs,
Got a surprise when they opened the front door to a ninety-two-year-old woman holding a revolver.

See, I told you, nobody better come for Ms. Johnston.
Don't nobody come for Ms. Johnston.

When you're living in a crime-ridden neighborhood and police nowhere can be seen to stand,
You do like Ms. Johnston and take your protection and safety into your own hands.
See, investigators weren't in uniform when they arrived,
She felt her life in danger and wasn't about to let these strangers inside.
They claimed they announced themselves after they opened the door,
But it was too little too late because
Ms. Johnston you weren't coming for.

Don't nobody come for Ms. Johnston.
Betta not come for Ms. Johnson.

She had her revolver ready and with a steady hand,
Ms. Johnston fired a couple of shots that hit three policemen.
Officers returned fire after Ms. Johnston had made her hits.
There was still an opportunity to deescalate the situation, but no one tried one bit.
Told you, don't come for Ms. Johnston unless you call ahead.
With all the recent attacks on elderly in this community, officers should have been thinking with their heads.

But the police officers said they were in the right place.
Undercover officers had purchased illegal drugs from a man earlier that day.
So they returned that evening to that same house to execute a no-knock warrant.
For her own protection and safety that revolver was meant;
Not expecting to get shot in her own
self-defense.

Ms. Johnston still did her own cooking and
cleaning and had a sharp mind.
They got it wrong and messed with the wrong
one this time.
Everybody on the block knows,
don't nobody come for Ms. Johnston.
Told 'em don't nobody come for
Ms. Johnston.
They didn't hear me though.
Don't nobody come for Ms. Johnston.

#ForKathrynJohnston

Why

Screams!
Signs!
Protests!
Shouts!
No answers to questions why
Mom holding a one-year-old had to die?

The baby was only one.
Based on suspicion,
SWAT goes in for a drug raid.
Door bashed,
Guns drawn,
Looking for the drug-dealing boyfriend;
Shots in the dark fired in a bedroom with her
and six kids.
Unnecessary loss of life for something somebody
else did.

Even *CSI*, *NCIS*, *Law & Order*, and the rest of
the cop shows
Show them taking surveillance, staking out the
environment,
Negotiating before acting like some super Rambo.
So firing three shots into room is deemed as
reckless,
Cop retains desk job, but still no real justice.
Settlement reached, but no admission of guilt.
Shot through a baby and killed his mama,
Ain't enough apologies that will heal this drama.

Screams!
Signs!
Protests!
Shouts!
Still no answers to the questions why!
Why we so hell-bent to take a black life?

#ForTarikaWilson

Bad Boys

Bad boys
Bad boys
Reggae beat
Sounding loud
Playing on repeat.

What I hear
In my ears,
See in my head,
Cops peaking around corners,
Guns drawn,
Breaking down doors,
Neighbors looking out windows in dread.

Bad Boys
Bad Boys
What they call the cops;
Community barely sees them but most often not.

But here's a chance to be a star,
Filming a reality show may get you far.
So to really set things off, you throw in a grenade,
Don't think to double-check the address, just go
by what the informant said.

Claim the grandma grabbed the officer's gun
In an effort to get your story right;
But how could that be,
Was she not stretched out on the far side of the
couch that night?

Bad boys
Bad boys

And you big and bold, kick open a door already
unlocked?
You threw a grenade so close to the child that it
burned the blanket.
So just go in commando with no knock-knock?
Pull out your weapon and with a single shot,
Strike a girl in the head exiting her neck,
And all you can do is call this event unfortunate?

Bad, bad, bad, bad boys
You're messing with human lives, not toys.
It's bad enough you got the wrong address;
No need to rush asking a community for
forgiveness.
Trigger-happy policeman, I hope you can sleep
the night through;
For the murder of a seven-year-old girl, who ain't
never done anything to you.

Bad boys
Bad boys
Just plain bad.

#ForAiyanaStanley-Jones

State of Mind

In a place of overcrowding,
In a place known for prisoners who inflict
self-harm,
No signs of counsel from the wise;
No signs of treatment protocols of any kind.

No diagnosis or therapy for the troubles faced in
our heads,
No signs of any help, yet a sister ends up dead.
Ring the bells, sound the alarm,
Send smoke signals for another colored girl gone.

I want to believe,
Hope to believe,
Need to believe,
There's safety for me,
There's justice for me,
That color is not a factor in respect of my
humanity.
Yet the system continues to cover its behind,
Makes the victim receive the blame time after
time.
Forget the act of self-defense against another
patient's sexual assault.
Forget the police officer relieved from duty due
to his prior violent assault.

Yet I the victim of the crime get blamed
Dig up my history and that's now how you say
my name.
So now people know about this alleged shoplifting
crime,
But no one cared about the state of mind.

Physical abuse.
Trauma that goes untreated,
Criminalization.
It's a violation of my human rights.
How do the perpetrators of abuse even sleep at
night?
Will truth one day arise and prevail?
Guess we'll know as more bodies are found dead,
dead in jail cells.

#ForSarahReed

Clear My Mind

Clear my mind,
Clear the clutter in my head.
Voices in surround sound
Encompassed by anxiety and dread.

No danger to anyone,
No threat of self-harm.
Just give me my space.
No need to call anyone.

They just don't understand.
See . . .
There's a high cost, for intervention
You call for medical attention.

Clear my mind
Off my meds
Four officers
Chased, in my own home
Scared to death.
Frightened, cornered
In a basement bedroom
Forced face down facing uncertain doom.

Clear my mind
Pressure applied
Handcuffed
Stopped breathing before the ambulance finally
arrived.

Clear my mind
Mom and sister saw it all,
But police records don't show their views,
Just the call.

If you lack the sensitivity to deal with a mental
situation,
Send in the team that has the training and
education.
Was just home trying to be me
In my space where I can be free.

Just to
Just to clear
Just to clear my
Just to clear my mind
Suffocated, can't breathe.

#ForShereeseFrancis

In the Chi

There's a history in the Chi
Shots get fired in the Chi
No one gets convicted in the Chi
Stories get twisted in the Chi.

Police abuse
Brutality
Harassment
Lack of service.

Gotta form your own watch in the Chi
Like an Afro Justice League in the Chi
To protect and serve the people of the Chi.

Take it to the west side
Party in the park
After dark
Noise complaint
Noise complaint
Off-duty officer arrives on the scene
Verbal altercation, you know what I mean.

He says, she says
My word, yours
Rude or aggressive
Calm or chill.

Shots fired with no delay
Shot in the hand
Shot in the head
Cop cleared and walks away.

Reckless
Intentional
Involuntary manslaughter
Another acquittal.

Another sister lost
Protests
Vigils
Remembrance of a life gone too soon
We say her name, Rekia Boyd
Westside Chicago.

#ForRekiaBoyd

Pick Up on Aisle

I need an associate to aisle 5
Associate to aisle 5
Customer needs assistance

Customer needs assistance
In Housewares
Can I get a CSM to Electronics?
I need a CSM to go to Electronics.

Just shopping the local Walmart with some
friends
Laughing, talking, looking until someone crazy
jumped in.

Approached us accusing us of shoplifting
No badge, no ID, tensions shifting.

So we just broke and bolted to the parking lot
It wasn't going down today. It just was not.

Associate to customer service
Associate to customer service to pick up returns
I need an associate to customer service.

Ummm . . .
Where's your blue vest and name tag?
Didn't they just call you?
Shouldn't you be pushing in the carts?
Aren't you supposed to be the friendly greeter
that we see when we walk in the mart?

Dude gets in his car, escalating a chase
For some alleged item from Walmart, he catches
a case.

So he fires, striking the perpetrator of this
unforgivable crime in the neck,
But of course, because the officer was between
the door and driver's seat he feared for his safety.

No thought was given for who else was in the car,
Now two young children have lost their mother.

Isn't there some protocol for why you give chase?
Some cheap good from the mart just unnecessary
waste.

Waste of time
Waste of resources
You off-duty man
So giving chase and catching the bad guy would
totally boost your career?

Family can't eat, can't sleep,
Unanswered questions just hanging in the air,
Couldn't even let the family see their daughter's
body.
These are the ones we trust to protect and care.

Can I get an associate?
Can I get a manager?
Can I get somebody?

Explain how you get from shopping to chase
Then from chase to death in your parking space.

No more shopping for a while,
Don't want to be the next pick up in the mart aisle.

#ForShellyFrey

Packed Tight

Cramped up like sardines,
And what does this mean?
For no rhyme or reason,
I just lose my humanity.

Thrown into a holding cell with fifteen others,
Pleas for help
Ignored by cops.
Protect and serve, who is that for?

Does this mean that you lock me in a cage?
Treat me like an animal?
Oblivious to the loud and boisterous bangs,
Just another alcoholic in pain.

So what do you do when you feel physically sick?
Officer threatens to lose your paperwork if you
don't silence things quick.
Order of protection, a fight with grandma
Resulting in the assault charge.

Two remotes and two tables broken,
Allegedly the result of a bottle of vodka.
Moved to another crammed cell on the next floor;
Fellow inmates see me placed on a bench,
convulsing even more.

Yet still officers turned aside, dismissing the shouts,
Like a seizure, it will pass, so let it play out.
Time passed before EMS was finally called,
Dead for twenty minutes prior, and not one officer took notice at all.

No matter how you tell it,
The response just wasn't right.
Guess it's not only the sardines,
That are packed too tight.

#ForKyamLivingston

U-Turn

Day off
Time off
Take a trip
Needed a lift.

Going to DC
Let's see what we can see
U-Turn
Child in tow
Snacks like Cheerios.

So much to see and do,
May see a friend or two.
Got a break from the dental-hygiene chair,
So ready to get there.

U-Turn
On roads, you don't really know,
Not sure which way to go,
Made turn at a checkpoint,
Guns were drawn—panic out of joint.

Backed into a squad car,
Not getting to far.
U-Turn
GPS got me into a mess,
In a traffic circle, now in distress.
Rammed barriers?
Breached perimeters?
Twenty-six shots fired,
The child in trauma, screaming, hungry, tired.

True answers we'll never know,
Police walk away like heroes,
Just another black woman dead and gone.
Life just moves on and on.
U-Turn

#ForMiriamCarey

Stuck

Stuck
Stuck
Now I don't give a
Tired of being in the middle of these fools,
Fussing and fighting is all they care to do.
Stuck
Stuck
I don't give a
Trying to separate them and keep the peace,
But who is in the middle all the time?
Yep, me.
Stuck
Stuck
I don't give a
So this madness stops today.
Dispute getting heated, dialed 911 right away.
Police yelling at me to come outside,
I'm not in the fight.
Get the man out front and the other one,
I ain't got nothing to hide.
Stuck
Stuck
I don't give a
So instead of really trying to see what he could see,
Soon as I open the door, two shots fired at me
You used your personal semiautomatic rifle:
Failure to comply?
All you were called to do was simply break up a
fight.
Blame it on the men in dispute that night,
Blame it on it being dark and having poor sight.

Didn't use his bulletproof vest or SUV for cover,
What was he thinking going into this problem?
So this is how it ends for those who do right?
Those who try to broker a peace in the middle of
the night?
Good, kind, gentle person is how I'd be described,
Just didn't know being stuck in the middle would
be the way I'd die.

#ForYvetteSmith

You Ain't Grown

I got your grown.
Four score, a decade plus three,
I got your grown.
Dress myself,
Feed myself,
Take care of my own home,
Go where I want to go.
Gonna take my keys?
Gonna take my keys?
Call the law cause I won't give you my keys?
You ain't grown.
What you know about the times I lived?
What you know about sacrifice?
What you know about making do?
What you know about canning and preserving?
What do you know about making a dollar and
meals stretch?
What? Huh? I ain't hear you saying nothing.
'Cause you ain't grown.
What I'm not gonna do is give up my keys.
What you're not gonna do is take away my dignity.
What I'm gonna do is fire this shot in the ground.
And maybe you'll know who runs this house here.
'Cause you ain't grown.
The officer didn't know me,
Just knew what my nephew said,
But only by officer's gun to be struck dead.
Grown Folks Actions

#ForPearlieGolden

Mind Matters

When you have high blood pressure,
They say cut out the salt.
When you have weight issues,
They say no flour, no sugar, and get rid of the
carbs.
When you have heart issues,
You say goodbye to old-school cooking oil and
real butter.
When you have lung issues,
They tell you to quit smoking.
But what about the matter of the mind?
You know, the things left unsaid;
Memories that replay like a broken record.
The checklists that never seem to get completed.
All the do-it-yourself projects,
Dishes in the sink,
Clothes in the wash, dry, fold;
Cobwebs, dusting to be done,
Trash to take out.
Bed to make.
Meds to take.
What about the matter of the mind?
Who calls to see if you're alright?
Who worries about your safety at night?
Who lets you know if your balance is off and
you're not wrapped too tight?
What about the matter of the mind?
So you might forget the seconds, minutes, hours.
Maybe days lead one into the other.
Did I bathe?
Did I take one every four hours or two every six?

The mind can get lost needing to find its way.
Troubled, sometimes perplexed throughout the day.
Yet on this day, mom made the call.
Needed to be checked into a facility,
Be taken care of and all.
Depressed, bipolar, suffering from schizophrenia.
This a crime-ridden area; don't you understand?
Strange folks bombarded my door, and I've got a hammer in hand.
Didn't ask no questions.
Didn't put me in no hold.
No concern for the state of my soul.
With no hesitation or look at the time,
Life lost for my state of mind.

#ForMichelleCusseaux

Got It

You have a badge,
You have a gun,
And for that simple reason, you can just barge in
anybody's home?
Doesn't matter the time,
Day or night,
Your glorified protect and serve motto
automatically gives you that right?
Got it
You can pack and bear arms on your hip,
But a knife inside my home causes you to flip?
My right to protect myself in my home infringed,
No welcome or ring of the doorbell, you just come
right on in.
Got it
Great how the media tends to dig up one's past.
Let's criminalize the victim, take the light off the
officer's ass.
Ninety days for shoplifting in Kroger; old
conviction for stealing some financial device.
Media trying to be like Santa, checking the list
not once but twice.
Got it
So dashboard cameras possibly didn't get any
footage.
And an officer's audio, for recording, was not on.
Thought the purpose of all that was for your own
protection.
So you come into someone's home and your life
feels threatened?
Got it

You can fire shots into somebody's space and feel
justified
Escalating a domestic dispute; rounds fired,
somebody has to die.
What happened to the training that taught you
how to break up a fight?
Where did you learn that killing a
forty-year-old woman, possibly mentally ill was
right?
Got it
Now you want to set up a commission?
Big woo hoo! Let's have a celebration!
Now you want to have some diversity training?
Yeah, that will get you the popular vote next
election.
Want to improve community relations?
Too little, too late to heal the situation.
Problem solved by administrative leave,
For the family, justice is never received.
Another sister, an artist, had to die,
Guess she didn't have the right to protect herself
with that knife.
Got it

#ForAuraRosser

Forcefield

Forcefield
Protective
Surrounding
Encompassing
Shield
Forcefield
Defense
Security
Physics' vector
Electromagnetic arc
Forcefield
Shields up
911 emergency
Domestic dispute
Within twenty seconds
From entering the front door
Break in the field
Couldn't wield the knife
Away from a fearful woman
In attack mode of her husband/fiancé
Mama tiger enraged
His side
Blame on her
No questions
Intentions unclear to officers
Assumptions made
Felt threatened
What happened to other means of disarmament?
Like one shot or a hold
Rapid response
Shots fired

Field down
Litigation pending
DA finds officer justified
Fatal shooting
Crack in the field
Break in the field
Shattered field
Useless field
Did not protect
Did not defend
Did not secure
Forcefield

#ForMeaganHockaday

You Ain't Know

You ain't know.
You ain't know.
Been on the streets since '09,
Taking care of business, doing fine.

You ain't know.
You ain't know.
Hair on fleek,
Makeup on point,
It's my sex you seek.
Don't get bent out of joint.

You ain't know.
You ain't know.
Heels high, skirt tight,
Flying high, styled right.
You weren't ready.

You just ain't know.
You ain't know about,
All this sway,
All this sashay,
All of this slay,
All day, every day.

You just ain't know.
Can I fault you for your ignorance?
Can I fault you for your crime?
Just me and my girl,
Taking a smooth ride.
But,

But I,
But I guess,
I made.
I made a,
I made a wrong,
I made a wrong turn,
Wrong turn.

Wrong turn too late,
Straight up crashed in the NSA gate.
Shots fired, can't hide
This was not how a woman's supposed to die.

But see, you ain't know.
This is how it goes down;
When the streetlights come on,
The dark side of town.

Just so you know,
So you know the truth,
The victim becomes the perpetrator
To protect the blue.
So we bring up the prior history.
The assault, the arrest,
Doesn't change the fact that it led to an unjustified
death.

I made
A wrong turn
Made a wrong turn
Wrong turn
Was the car really stolen,
Or did the "john" not pay up?
Could have been the car owner's drugs,
Have him take a lie detector or pee in a cup.

You ain't know.
You ain't know.
Made a wrong turn and lost my way,
You ain't know.
You ain't know.
Every night on these streets I slay,
You ain't know.
You ain't know.
Choices bad too often made,
You ain't know.
You ain't know.
My life was not meant to end this way.

#ForMyaHall

Transparency

Ability to see through
Obvious
Manifestation
Recognizable
Distinct
Can be detected
Transparent
Asked for
Begged for
Demanded
Marching for
Protesting for
Questions in search of answers
Transparency
Handcuffed in the back of a squad car
MMM HMMM.
Died?
Sho' Nuff.
Can't get outside investigators?
No perspective on this whole situation?
Say so.
She slipped out of the cuffs.
Fired a pistol at officers.
You don't say?
Wouldn't you have discovered a pistol?
Like,
Once cuffed,
Duh!
Transparency
Another—
Victim.

Another victim
Another victim becomes
Another victim becomes perpetrator
Guilty
At fault
Blamed
Justice
Transparency
Transparency
Justice
Release the surveillance
Patrol car dash cam video
Security cameras
Cellphone footage
Release it
Transparency
Need to know the truth
The truth of it all
For all to see
Can there just be
Transparency

#ForAlexiaChristian

I Can't

I can't say I didn't know.
I can't say I didn't expect.
I can't say I didn't have my fingers crossed.
Hoping,
Praying,
Believing,
Protesting,
Marching,
Keeping vigil,
Meditating,
Screaming,
Crying
For justice,
For truth,
For sanity,
For brown and black bodies,
For peace;
But like a slap in the face,
I get unanswered questions.
Like a slap in the face,
I can't claim my rights.
Like a slap in the face,
My question of authority becomes assault.
Failure to signal,
Like a slap in the face,
Swung elbow and kicked his shins?
From inside the car;
Ordered out the car.
Charged with assault.
Slap in the face.
I can't.

I can't understand the who.
I can't understand the what.
I can't understand the why.
Hung in a cell by a garbage bag deemed suicide.
What?
I can't.
New job,
New life,
Fresh start,
Now silenced,
I can't breathe.
I can't function.
I can't make sense of it all.
Depression,
Mental state of mind,
Can't stop wondering,
Can't stop worrying.
Can't stop the nerves.
Can't stop the anxiety.
Being a brown girl,
Wrapped in brown skin,
I can't speak my mind,
Without you feeling threatened?
Are you that soft?
I can't.
Everywhere I go,
Being watched,
Like an animal being preyed upon.
Can't work.
Can't play.
Can't love.
Can't pray.
Still trying to claim my 2/5,
This is too much.
In search of sacred space,

Need a resting place;
For my weary soul.
I can't.

#ForSandraBland

Sweet Sixteen

Games
Tryouts
Clubs
Learner's permit
License
Part-time/Summertime or no-time job
PSAT
SAT Prep
Sweet sixteen
Homecoming
Dances
Dates
Friends
Hanging out
Sweet sixteen
Parent confrontation
Detention center
Refusal to remove sweatshirt
Aikido-style restraint
No response to food offers or call from mom
Strange
Sweet sixteen
Found
Dead
Locked room
Alone
In her sleep
Breathed her last
Sudden cardiac arrhythmia
What possible triggers
Mystery

Sweet sixteen
Investigation
Employees faulted
Bed check on the regular—failed
Falsifying logs
People do that?
Call for reform
Plans for change
Retraining
Sweet sixteen
Three fired
Two Indicted
Pleaded not guilty
Mama filed suit
Claims staffer watched
No assistance provided
As she struggled
As she gasped for air
As she suffered a seizure
No lavish invitations
No grand entrance
No surprise guest performance
No cake, balloons
No friends and family
No fancy party dress
No amazing ride donning a bow to ride off into
the night
Sweet sixteen

#ForGynnyaMcMillen

Who Will Speak?

Who will speak on behalf of the dead?
When there's been no pre-needs plan.
No church,
No funeral home selected.
No Old/New Testament scriptures,
No hymns or solos,
No plans to write obituaries.
No acknowledgments,
No two-minute limit for words from community,
friends or family
Who will speak on behalf of the dead?
Questions still unanswered
Timeline doesn't match up
Felt threatened
At an intersection
A parked car
Five officers
A barrage of bullets released,
into a car.
Who will speak on behalf of the dead?
Mother of three boys dead on the scene
Father of four girls dies later in the hospital
Victims become the perpetrators of their own
demise
Blood alcohol levels, presence of ADHD type
meds in system
Stopped car
Parked car
No response
So you use bullets to de-escalate?
Lack of transparency

Gives no confidence in those who have led
Who will speak on behalf of the dead?
Gathering outside city hall
Voices in protest
Plans to voice concerns
Calling for satisfaction
Council meeting gets canceled
Who will speak for the dead?
Can we get a status report?
Can you release all recordings from the morning
of the shooting?
Can we terminate the officers involved?
Can we recommend charges to the DA?
Can we provide a fund for the children of the
deceased?
Who will speak for the dead?
Thirteen shots fired into the body of a mother –
in a parked car
Discipline results are confidential
Officers no longer on the force
Insufficient answers
Who will speak for the dead?
Who will speak for the . . .
Who will speak for . . .
Who will speak?
Who?
Will you?

#ForKishaMichael

My Own

I've got my own.
Space
Place
A spot where I can create.
I've got my own
Man
Plan
Beautifully brown
Hot damn.
I've got my own
Goals
Dreams
Hopes, so it seems.
I've got my own
Beauty, shines like the stars
Don't need your ride
Got my own car.
I've got my own.
But you don't think.
No,
You don't believe.
No,
You don't check to see.
No,
You just presume.
Yes,
Can't conceive – yes.
Yes
That someone of my skin tone
Has got her own.
Yet, I threatened your safety

But you gunning for me?
Yeah,
You didn't know,
The girl's got her own.
Yeah, you can run and resign;
But unarmed murder is never justified.
Best believe true colors have truly been shown.
Folks still can't believe that we've got our own.

#ForJessicaWilliams

That Melanin

Black girl, black girl
Brown girl, brown girl
Curly, natural, wavy, hair bone straight
Sun-kissed
Caramel-coated
Head high
Body-sculpted.
Strong, proud
Quiet, loud
Sometimes misbehaving
Baby-raising
Working
Trying to make it
Warrants
Traffic violation
Became a standoff situation
Storm my home, my space
My kids, I can't protect the sanctuary of my own place.
Guess there was too much brown
No attempts to de-escalate, just fire around
Yeah, shades of color put you on an endangered list.
This is what happens when you're not melanin-deficient.
That melanin will get you pulled over.
That melanin will get your hands up,
Still shot.
That melanin will get you choke held
Can't breathe.
No hesitation

No de-escalation
Shots fired round after round
Oh, it's just a toy.
Damn –
That melanin
Got me looking over my shoulder
Peeping round corners
No jaywalking
Be careful whose yard you're crossing
That melanin
Have your gun on hand to protect your home and
child
Trying to video for the record
Did it capture it all?
Some, but not enough
Will you see the truth, hear the truth,
Know the truth?
That melanin
Have you shouting loud
What you not gonna do is come up in here
Threatening mine
Shots fired
Child cradled
All because of that melanin
That melanin
That damn melanin

#ForKorrynGaines

Hate Crime

Hate
The hate you dish out,
The hate you can't take.
The hate that fuels the system,
The hate that makes justice wait.
The hate with two sets of laws,
With no demand to do what is right;
Fueling the rhetoric that social media now brings
to light.
The hate that erases evidence from the scene,
Changes the nature of the story;
Victim becomes predator in the scheme.
The hate that says look, act, and be like me,
White skin, blue eyes, this is perfection you see,
Because nothing can be beautiful about shades
of brown,
Nothing of value in you, in your culture or
worship to be found.
So remove your hijab,
Take on our Western ways;
Eat our food, speak our language, and you will
live yet another day.
The hate, intimidated by young women wearing
abayas,
Girls gathered in laughter, food, and fellowship
before the sunrise.
The hate that murders without being called a
crime,
Struck by a metal bat, assaulted, taken in a car;
Dumped in a pond,
But call it road rage.

A community mourns in midst of prayers and its
holy days.
An act motivated by racial, sexual, or other
prejudice is how we define a hate crime,
Why can't you see this act as what it is?
Will we ever get this justice thing right?
It's way past time.

#ForNabraHassanen

Call to Work

We are sisters in our sacred space,
Let all the world be silent around us.
Our feet shall stand in solidarity and peace, Oh,
America;
I was glad when they said to me, let us come
together and work.

#TheBrothers

4WHAT IS MAN, THAT THOU ART
MINDFUL OF HIM? AND THE SON OF
MAN, THAT THOU VISITEST HIM?
5FOR THOU HAST MADE HIM A
LITTLE LOWER THAN THE ANGELS,
AND HAST CROWNED HIM WITH
GLORY AND HONOUR.
6THOU MADEST HIM TO HAVE
DOMINION OVER THE WORKS OF
THY HANDS; THOU HAST PUT ALL
THINGS UNDER HIS FEET:

PSALMS 8:4–6 (KJV)

Pre-Message Selection

Repent, for the kingdom of heaven is at hand
Repent, for the kingdom of heaven is at hand
Repent, for the kingdom of heaven is at hand

Cries out the prophet John in the wilderness
To turn men from their sin and wickedness
Preparing a people for the coming salvation
To give them hope in the midst of chaos and
destruction

Repent, for the kingdom of heaven is at hand
Repent, for the kingdom of heaven is at hand
Repent, for the kingdom of heaven is at hand

Prophets from that time to now cry out across
the lands
Begging the sinner to turn from his wicked ways
and come to God once again
Yet as many messengers have been sent
But of this one sin, many cannot repent

Repent, for the kingdom of heaven is at hand
Repent, for the kingdom of heaven is at hand
Repent, for the kingdom of heaven is at hand

This one sin that has you seeing the difference
in color
That claims superiority, when we're all God's
children, sisters and brothers,
The sin that wants a religion to claim
Yet disrespects people of color, calling them out
of their name

Repent, for the kingdom of heaven is at hand
Repent, for the kingdom of heaven is at hand
Repent, for the kingdom of heaven is at hand

This selfish sin only serves to benefit them
Not willing to see the humanity of others or their
own privilege
You can call it separate but equal,
Integrate and question why we demand more?

Repent, for the kingdom of heaven is at hand
Repent, for the kingdom of heaven is at hand
Repent, for the kingdom of heaven is at hand

Your unwanted properties become our ghettoes
Living in a vast food desert where nothing healthy
can be purchased or grows
Communities riddled with violence and crime
Yet you take no share of the blame, not one single
time

Repent, for the kingdom of heaven is at hand
Repent, for the kingdom of heaven is at hand
Repent, for the kingdom of heaven is at hand

The blood of many yet cries from the ground
Second class access to jobs and education
abounds
But we never can seem to get the stats right
While you bombard the media with false stereotypes
Controlling what you want all to believe
When in truth it is you yourselves who are greatly
deceived

Repent, for the kingdom of heaven is at hand
Repent, for the kingdom of heaven is at hand
Repent, for the kingdom of heaven is at hand

For if you humble yourselves and pray
Wholeheartedly turn from wicked ways
God will hear and heal our land
Until that happens on shaky ground we all stand
The hope of salvation and the joy it represents
Can be had if we in humility acknowledge our sin
and repent

Repent, for the kingdom of heaven is at hand
Repent, for the kingdom of heaven is at hand
Repent, for the kingdom of heaven is at hand

Emmett Till

Every summer, this is how it goes
We had that talk before I sent him down the road.
He knows how to speak, what to say and do.
The South is a different place, not what you're used to.
Don't look at them directly in the eyes,
If you see them coming on the sidewalk, be sure to step aside.
In their stores, they'll let you spend what you can,
They'll never put your change directly in your hand.
To ride the bus, you'll pay your fare up front, but instead of going right through,
You get off and go through the door at the back and end up standing if you have to.
Just mind your manners and pay attention to what your kin have to say,
Not sending you down to visit my family to put me to shame.
Don't go down there to my people and act like you don't have home training,
Mississippi ain't like the south side of Chicago this is a different trip.
You're going to encounter a level of hatred, hopefully I've prepared you for it.
You've got to take care Emmett because I know you like pulling pranks,
But these are hard times for our people, and Mississippi is not the place

Outside the country store, bragging to cousins
and friends about having a white girlfriend back
to home,
They dare him to ask the white woman behind
the counter for a date, teasing and egging him on.
Emmett, a smooth-talking teen goes in to buy
some candy and leaves saying bye baby,
There were no witnesses in the store,
but it doesn't take much to make the
white folks go crazy.
The woman behind the counter would go on to
claim that Emmett grabbed her,
whistled at her, and made lewd advances.
The woman's husband, back from business,
enraged by what happened decided to round up
a crew, not taking any chances.
So they go to the home of Emmett's
great-uncle demanding to see the boy
Despite the pleas of the family,
Emmett is forced into the car.
Driving around all night, traveling near, not too far,
They beat Emmett behind a residence.
Taking him down to the river;
hearts full of hate, no repentance.
Three days later Emmett's corpse was recovered,
so disfigured, not a human being
The only way his great uncle could identify his
body was by an initialed ring.
Local authorities wanted to bury him quickly and
quietly put the story away,
Mama requested the body come home to Chicago
without delay.
After seeing her boy's mutilated remains,
Funeral arrangements had to be made.

With a strong will and faith, Mamie Till didn't assign another to task this,
She made a brave decision to make it an open casket.
She wanted Jim Crow, segregation, and racial hatred to be exposed,
She wanted the world to see and know what they did to her boy.
Two weeks following the burial, the case went to trial,
Given an all-white jury, you knew this wouldn't take a while.
Despite witnesses positively identifying the killers,
It took less than an hour for the jury to deliberate and come back with a not guilty verdict.
People across the country about the decision were outraged,
This case laid the groundwork for the Civil Rights Movement in the coming days.
Time moves on and continues telling our oral and written history,
Of a time where having, black or brown skin was a dangerous thing to be.
In later years, with all players nearly dead and gone, news would be uncovered
The woman at the center of it all confesses she lied, and the truth is discovered.
No charges, no indictment, or settlement would ever be given
No satisfaction for the dead, but the burden becomes ours to do all the forgiving

What began as a talk that mothers gave then,
now, and always will,
From that time going forward end with,
Remember what happened to Emmett Till

#ForEmmettTill

Savages Just Savages

It amazes me, still amazes me
How resilient a people could be.
Stolen from a land that was unknown
To become another man's property, with no place
to call home.
Slow death to original language, tribe, and
custom,
And no way to get back to where we came from.
Yet for not being learned of your foreign ways,
We were identified and called savages, chained
and beaten slaves.
Like an animal, we were checked, branded, and
berated,
Only three-fifths human, your precious
constitution stated.
Yet we work your land, building, planting and
doing the things you should have done,
Yet you have the nerve to label us savage, every
single one.
Since those times the stories haven't changed,
Same stereotyped images and human dignity
delayed.
This was the story of Abner Luoima, a black
Haitian immigrant,
At his home, he was an electrical engineer, but
now a security guard in Brooklyn.
To a popular night spot Club Rendez-Vous he
goes,
Got caught in the middle of a fight between two
women along with fellow party goers.

Among the first cops on the scene incorrectly identified Luoima of giving him a sucker punch of all things.

If Luoima had been the one who'd thrown it, he probably wouldn't have been able to so quickly respond, know what I mean?

But because this officer couldn't take a hit, a spirit of savagery took over him;

Leading him and all of the officers to beat the man with two-way radios, fists, and nightsticks.

The madness did not just end there, but once at the precinct the cops, drunk with anger,

Dragged Louima into the bathroom while they kicked and squeezed his privates, putting him in grave danger.

They proceeded to take a plunger handle and sexually assaulted Louima.

He'd require three surgeries for his colon and bladder, according to the nurse in the emergency room.

He remained in the hospital two months, while outside the case received local and national attention.

And these savages had the nerve to plead not guilty, but tunes started to change midway point of the trial,

As the bevy of charges mounted civil right violations, obstruction of justice, false statements; if I listed more you'd be reading for a while.

So one savage was found guilty, sentenced to thirty years without parole.

The one who assisted this cop in the bathroom only got fifteen years from what the news told.

The other officers were indicted but due to insufficient evidence,

Avoided prison time and a lengthy sentence.
Louima would sue the city and receive an $8.75 million dollar settlement,
The largest settlement in NYC history and haven't heard of any bigger since.
The stereotypical image of the savage they want you to see:
A black man, barely clothed, naked with bones through his nose and jagged teeth.
The truth of the image is never shown, and so stereotypes people continue to believe.
The brutality against the humanity of a people has become the norm more so than average,
As more pictures, recordings, and videos show the faces of these savages, just savages.

#ForAbnerLouima

The Reach

Unarmed with no criminal record of to speak,
Forty-one shots fired because of what police
thought he was trying to reach.
Isn't it typical for officers to request ID?
To accurately identify the subject before arresting?
But not out of certainty but operating on a hunch,
Thought he fit the description of a man wanted
for rape, yeah right, thanks a bunch.
Oh, thank you, officers, our community is now
further safe.
You took the life of a harmless street peddler who
just sold his goods every day.
The guy did not give chase and take off and run,
He was simply standing in his complex, but you
mistook his reach, as a reach for a gun
Hands outstretched, visible so the eyes can see,
Going into my pocket to let you know my identity.
From a day of hard work, tired and just making
it through,
Decided to go downstairs and gather my thoughts
in the vestibule
Just a reach into a pocket, ill perceived,
Posed no threat, but a threat was believed.
Could they have not just in one shot incapacitated
the threat?
One bullet in the leg to uncover the truth that
they were meant to seek.
Yet for doing the unthinkable these insecure and
overzealous officers are praised,

Even getting a promotion without any form of disciplinary actions, the question by the victim's mother is raised.

All he was trying to do was save money for college, Had saved almost $9,000 to attain an opportunity for expanding his knowledge.

Yet a dream deferred this would be, Forty-one bullets of mistaken identity.

Just for the reach.

#ForAmadouDiallo

Settlement

The settlement is an agreement.
Terms reached with, side A and side B
Does not consider wrongdoing on either sides part,
Just a way to silence the riots and protests and everyone gets their part.
So they come to the table side A and side B.
Call side A, the officers and side B, the family.
An unarmed black teen is murdered according to side B.
Side A will ever stick to its claim of feeling threatened, now do you see?
Since the news of the tragedy spread through the media like wildfire,
Riots and protests take over the city; the racial tension couldn't get any higher.
So a three-month-old boy will now grow up without a father.
Side A shows no remorse or concern and acts unbothered.
From this table, neither side can leave,
Until terms of agreement can be reached.
This process can go for however long,
Both sides hold to their opinions, standing strong.
Just another tall black male suspect,
Dispatcher says he's got fourteen open warrants.
So a chase begins, the suspect runs,
Police officer spots him, swears suspect is reaching for a gun.
So he fires the bullet before the end of the night,

Piercing the suspect's heart, and identity comes to light.

He was just a nineteen-year-old young father with an infant son,

No gun was ever found at the scene, not a single one.

So like a lit match, the city explodes,

Got riot police marching through the streets with tear gas and a reign of terror to impose.

Warrants for a nonviolent offense, what could it be? Can you even suppose?

Stopped by several different officers within the same day—driving without a license, see how it goes?

You enter the zone of the officers who never forget pulling you over for a simple ticket,

Yet based on the word from dispatch, you soon become a moving target.

So continued meetings at the table between side A and side B,

Then after much deliberation, terms are finally reached.

While the media may reveal an approximate payout amount,

The dollars and cents barely matter when for a life, the other, takes no account.

Almost seems like hush money to silence the tide,

To keep people in their place and from not speaking out against the injustices the city continues to hide.

So they get up from the table to go their separate ways,

To live and breathe another day, side B and side A.

Justice cries will yet come from the streets, let's
not forget
Everything didn't get answered when both sides
reached a settlement.

#ForTimothyThomas

Party Invitation

Nothing like a special party, it's a beautiful celebration.
What makes a party more personal is when you receive that invitation.
The invitation is exclusive to you,
Sometimes you get to bring a guest, and sometimes that won't do.
The invitation gets you excited about your upcoming plans,
You think of how you're going to dress and be center of attention.
In a big city, you may hop around a place downtown or two,
But the most hype parties are the ones at the cribs where all the guys and the girls come through.
What's a weekend without an event to socialize?
Hang out with friends, to eat, dance, listen to music and have a good time.
If you thought a party with off-duty police officers would somehow be safe,
You have another thing coming if you read or heard about this case.
From stripping at the bachelorette party to the pub, these guys go along
A party on the south side of Milwaukee, what could possibly go wrong?
So it's early in the a.m. when this odd group arrives,
The party had been going on for hours, and there was a lot of alcohol inside.

This mixed group of white women and then 2
black guys
Regardless of their varying shades of blackness,
they received the shade and side eye.
Hearing the music playing, this is going to be
some party too,
But you could hear a pin drop when the new
company was introduced.
It was like everyone stopped what they were
doing to take a look
At this group of new arrivals, and so they must
have been spooked.
You see somebody misread the communication.
They should have been clear on who their plus
one could be on their invitation.
The two women went off to the bathroom, and
then everything starts to go down,
The men are approached by the host, an off-duty
officer, followed by another guest to intimidate
and surround.
When the girls return the guys told them they felt
uncomfortable.

Did they know if the host and his guests were
racist? The decision was to make an exit out the
door.
They headed to get into the truck, and the crowd
surrounds and forms.
Accused them of taking a police badge and from
there, the arguing goes back and forth.
Doesn't make sense to call the cops or dial 911,
One had punched the truck's headlamp as the girl
handed her bag for inspection.
Two young black men in mixed company going to
an unknown party,

Talk about a case of stranger danger and being aware of your surroundings.

Harris was pulled from the truck by two men shouting racial slurs,

One of the crowd sliced his cheek before he broke free and took off.

Jude was also pulled out the truck despite protesting that he'd done nothing wrong,

It quickly became a mob scene like hate-filled flashbacks of long ago.

They punched and kicked this guy, yelling and screaming to accuse.

"Who took my badge, where's my badge?" Nothing but confusion.

There were people laughing, standing to the side as they ripped Jude's pants,

They demanded to know where Harris, the other 'N- - - -r' went.

Man was beaten, and the cops called the cops,

Who handcuff him because they were told that the man was resisting arrest.

The images are so gruesome it will take away your breath.

Jude wasn't taken to the hospital by ambulance,

He was treated like a criminal and taken by the police wagon.

Until the police were gone, Jude wouldn't say a word,

Photos of injuries were taken, Jude was treated; his side finally heard.

Still accused of taking an officer's badge,

Jude and Harris were picked up later and for suspicion of the theft held.

While the party host and three other officers were suspended from the force,

When it came time for justice the criminal probe was stalled.

Given the beat down that Jude received,

How did you expect him to identify his attackers when he was beaten to the point of barely able to see?

The women could only pick out a couple people from the line-up, but weren't certain if they were the ones hitting Jude,

So the investigators then had to rely on help from the other cops in blue.

So months passed with no charges filed; an ongoing mess,

Then the blue wall of silence was broken, and officer and his partner became key witnesses.

In the state trial, the jury acquitted the three officers charged,

The outrage and the demand for justice caused protests to enlarge.

Then we make it to the federal investigation and let's see what they did,

The federal grand jury convicted three officers who were originally acquitted.

Now they did acquit the fourth officer,

Just a little bit of justice is all we asked for.

No stolen badge was ever discovered, nor was resisting arrest the true situation,

Just didn't understand the party invitation.

#ForFrankJudeJr.

Chillin'

Just chillin' with my boys,
Chillin' with my boys,
Clowning, talking smack,
Not making serious noise.
Just jonning on each other reflecting on the day,
School, girls, cars and the latest video games.
Going to the movies or hanging at a mall,
Talking about our number one pick and when
we're gonna make that call.
Chillin', yeah chillin',
Yeah, just chillin' with my boys.
No big plans or what not,
Just in the car in the parking lot.
Then a light outta nowhere starts shining in the car,
Driving off and away but didn't get very far.
Security guards doing rounds never to us
themselves identified
They could have been anybody meaning harm,
but instead they fired shots
Just chillin', yeah chillin',
Just chillin' with my boys.
You thought we were driving toward you, so it
was a threat, so you thought,
Even though the car veered in another direction
the gun firing didn't stop.
Charges filed against the officers but were soon
dismissed
Bullets flying, shot in the back, no one expected
the night to end like this
Just chillin' with my boys

#ForTravaresMcGill

Rule

After the last bell rings,
Teachers don't get to shout, dance and sing,
Nor do they kick back and listen to favorite CDs,
Staying late for staff meetings and those notorious PDs.
They pour over their desks with lesson plans, cleaning up manipulatives that fell out of small hands.
They come in early and leave the building late,
Stay up checking papers and putting in grades.
But after you put your time in, get your watch and give a speech,
You sign your retirement papers and head for crystal blue waters and a white sandy beach.
But for some, responsibilities beyond the classroom stay on the mind,
This was the case of Robert Davis, who traveled to check on property once left behind.
Wasn't too long ago when New Orleans was ravaged by that great storm,
Mr. Davis had returned to check on the property his family owned.
He went out that night looking to buy some cigarettes,
What ended up happening was a night he'd never forget.
Police alleged that Davis was publicly intoxicated; a charge he vehemently denied,
Hadn't had a drink in twenty-five years, as the incident played out that night.
He was resisting arrest, as they often like to say,

They didn't count on a news producer catching the confrontation on videotape.

A beating that began with just verifying the curfew, Officer interrupts a conversation, and then punches started to come through.

Davis starts to cross the street, but before he can complete the task,

Officer attacks and proceeds to tell him, I'll kick your a**.

Now what kind of language is that coming from an officer of the law?

His duty is to protect and serve, not to provide a violent beat down like some boxing match he once saw.

The charges against a retired teacher the officer manage to pile high,

Public intoxication, resisting arrest, battery on a police officer and public intimidation, so their actions they say were justified?

The beating left Davis having to have stitches beneath his left eye,

Back soreness, shoulder aches, and bandaged left hand that should heal in time.

Do unto others as you would have them do to you was what I learned at school,

Just seems like there some authorities that need to learn and apply the rule.

#ForRobertDavis

Toast

A toast.
A simple salutation,
A parade of shared jokes made into a speech.
Words of congratulations,
Good wishes for the present and the future;
From close family and friends from whom you've
received nurture.
A toast.
Appreciation for friendship over the years or job
well done,
A remembrance down memory lane, all the good,
the bad, the fun.
An honor to one whom celebration is meant,
A joyful act one sentiment.
A toast.
And in spirited homage glasses are raised,
Some filled just with a little taste, or to the rim
to need a ride home later that day.
A venue, filled with laughter and the sounds of
glasses clinking,
An act which is followed by happy people
drinking.
A toast.
Yet that would not happen on this wedding day,
A bride lost her groom in a most heinous and
dreadful way.
See the night before they each go with friends to
celebrate and do what they do:
Bachelorette party for the bride, and a bachelor
party for the groom.
So to the strip club, the groom and friends go.

Fight breaks out,
Next, come police in plain clothes.
The groom Sean and his crew make a dash,
getting into the car,
Not wanting to get caught in the madness, but an
accidental car swipe led to a bullet barrage.
A barrage of bullets, not just one, two, or three
Into the car of unarmed black men, even with
closed eyes you can envision the scene.
Couldn't stop, wouldn't stop at one, two or three,
They kept firing until the total was fifty.
Some officers walk away with forced retirement
and a pension,
Others remain employed with only one
terminated as a prime example.
Yet nothing the system can do will bring Sean's
life back,
A young father and groom too, about that family
life and on track.
So today the day everything was set,
But what was joy becomes grief, the loss we will
not soon forget.
With glasses raised, police brutality continually
exposed,
To no more hashtags, I raise this toast.

#ForSeanBell

This Ain't Laser Tag

This requires more strategy than the game we
used to play,
No ducking, dodging, hiding behind trees until
the streetlights came on, as back in the day.
This modern-day game requires more strategy
and skill,
It uses guns that fire infrared beams.
Each player wears some kind of vest or silly thing,
No freeze or running around saying tag you're it,
You get shot by a laser, and you know you've
been hit.
But this wasn't a game of tag at some indoor
arena,
Where you strategize with your team with only a
few barriers in between you.
Just call it a routine traffic stop,
The teen posed no danger, but the cops pursued
him on foot.
So he got confronted, and he ran and dodged into
an abandoned building.
Pronounced dead shortly after he was tasered,
Police claim they only fired once, but no, not like
a laser.
See when you play tag, you prep for the game,
Do research on your arena and come up with
strategic plays.
You dress appropriately for play so that in the
environment you blend,
You familiarize yourselves with the rules, because
you're playing to win.
You go in quickly to get the lay of the land,

You know your gun and find a good spot to fire from and stand.
You look for flashing lights so you can see what's coming toward you,
You quickly aim and start shooting, because racking up the points is what you want to do.
But this case was an unnecessary one,
He was a nonviolent teen, with not even a driver's license.
Why did he run away that night?
It's said he was a special education student and may have run out of fright.
Without explanation, not one officer could explain,
The level of aggression to chase this young man.
Chronologically sixteen but developmentally ten or eleven,
Description given of her grandson casting shadows on officers suggestion.
The teen didn't have a chance to aim for the zone or think offensively,
He didn't get a chance to run and find cover to evade his enemy.
He ran into a space trying not to be spotted,
Despite his valiant efforts by a single taser he was assaulted.
He didn't have a group of friends to discuss the strategy,
No opportunity to debrief for next time of play.
More than shocking the nervous system,
More than a five-second charge,
A teen's life got cut short today sending another community up in alarm.
Another black down, no need, this ain't no reason to brag.
This was a young man's life, no this ain't laser tag.

#ForRobertMitchell

Always

Always faithful
Always loyal
Always truthful
Always supportive
Faithful to God.
Loyal to country and the corps
Truthful in order to be made free.
Supportive of Family
Always
Served my country with great pride
Patriotism magnified
Yet with years served over time
It messes with your body and plays games with
your mind
Got a touch of respiratory issues
Got a touch of arthritis
Got a touch of bipolar
Not one for much drama or fuss
Always
Pendant around the neck in case of emergency
Just press a simple a button a rescue will be sent
immediately
Not meaning to, but on this day
Accidentally pushed the alert
The operator asked if I were okay
Didn't respond right away, so what to do?
Cops and ambulance are sent to my rescue
Always
I finally respond with an okay
Operator tries to intercept, but by then the team
had already left

Officers charge banging on the door after saying
I'm okay, they can leave
But they just wouldn't go, and barge in they did
proceed
Scared for my life, do I need to protect myself?
What am I to do?
Shouting, screaming, yelling, and then the racial
slurs
Loud enough to alert the neighbors; the operator
still on even heard
Just so you know, he said she says is how the cops
took their stand
They were only doing their jobs, the victim came
at them with knife in hand
Always
Taunted by slurs, tasered to subdue
Could the situation get any more escalated, were
these cops not through?
No pleas to leave would this terror stop
Even after beanbag rounds, a single bullet fired
the fatal shot
Always
Always faithful
Always loyal
Always truthful
Always supportive
To God, country, family, and the corps
With my last breath always
Even in death
Always

#ForKennethChamberlain

Just Stand

In the military process, you are called to stand at attention,
Ready to receive the next orders as they are mentioned.
School students stand, hands over hearts at daily command,
To pledge allegiance to the flag and to the republic for which it stands.
You just stand.
You stand in line for tickets to your favorite band's concert,
You stand in protest and remembrance of those you've seen murdered or hurt,
You stand to speak for those without voice,
You stand for the rights of others to make their own life's choice.
You just stand.
But when your life is threatened and there's nowhere to turn,
You're down for a visit, with a bag of Skittles and Arizona tea you're armed.
Yeah, you're walking through the neighborhood, and it's late at night,
Do I stop because somebody's yelling and screaming at me trying to give a fright?
You just stand.
Don't I have the right to stand my ground?
So I can't protect my own body when shots begin to sound?
It's okay for a black teen-aged boy in a hoodie to be attacked,

Yet that same boy can't stand up for himself and fight back.
STAND.
So for myself, I make a line in the sand,
A line to solidify where I stand,
A line that should not be crossed,
That says I am a man, no massa boss.
Just stand.
But true to form, what do I see?
That in America, its Bill of Rights doesn't cover me.
For everyone else, justice can be quickly found,
But you are out of luck if your skin is black or brown.
STAND.
From Douglass, Dubois, Washington, and even to the dream of King,
We have stood marching arm in arm, crying for justice not realizing what it would mean.
It's like a seed, in death is buried in the ground,
When nurtured and watered, new life is found.
And that seed of life begins to grow,
Marches, protests, and movements of solidarity we now come to know.
Just stand.
The dreams of my parents and my own I would not live to see,
Yet for those who follow let my legacy be,
That even though my life was hushed in death,
Don't allow silence to be the mark of your last breath.
STAND.

#ForTrayvonMartin

You Lie

Please don't think you can explain away,
Justifying murder, for in your heart are racists
ways.
Just call it stand your ground,
Until caught in a bold-faced lie you're found.
Just teens listening to their music a little loud,
Stopped at a gas station, not in some neighborhood
crowd.
So what gave you the right to even approach them
that way?
Tell them to turn their music down, why didn't
you just get your gas and pay?
But no, something inside you compelled you
because it was your inalienable right,
You had the right to confront these teens and
demand they follow your order just because
you're white.
Ten bullets you fired, claiming you feared for
your life.
Fired into a Durango of four teens, and in court,
on the Bible, you lie:
Saying Jordan threatened to kill you,
Reached for something, grabbed a 4-inch barrel
shotgun and aimed at you.
Then if that wasn't enough you embellish a little
more,
Saying that Jordan reached and opened the
vehicle door.
Too much of a tangled web you weaved,
When standing your ground you were determined
to deceive.

Yet the truth would be told,
A gas station patron heard the defendant say,
"You're not going to talk to me that way."
No one heard anyone in the Durango answer
back to what he had to say.
Neither did Jordan leave the vehicle or were their
weapons inside, the passengers in the vehicle
testified.
You felt threatened, you testified, when you're
the one that held the gun and with shots fired a
young black life that mattered died.
With deliberate intent, you planned to deceive,
Both judge and jury you wanted them to believe
That your life was in danger, this was so true,
You just couldn't handle the loud music and had
something to prove.
Intentional you were in forging ahead with your
falsehood,
Convicted of murder sentenced to life in prison
without parole for good.
For once, untruth was not justified,
Moral of the story, you can't get away with a lie.

#ForJordanDavis

Now You Know

If you don't know
Big brother
Strong brother
About my business
I ain't like no other,
For what you need, I've got it like a cure.
I'm not your average hustler, I'm a modern-day
entrepreneur.
By any means necessary, I'm determined to
succeed.
Ducking, dodging, or selling untaxed goods,
providing for a need;
Yeah, for the first time, the cops give you a
warning,
But I got a handle on my business; have a family
that depends on me.
If you don't know
Here comes a police car unmarked,
Here come the officers just something trying to
start.
Being about my business, I'm just selling
cigarettes,
Sometimes it's just a simple puff that can calm
and lift one's spirit.
Seriously, I told these officer dudes just to
back off,
Waving my arms frantically, but they continued
their approach.
No, you ain't going to detain me,
I'm not the one to be frisked,
If there's an issue, you read me my rights,

Then follow protocol and handle your business.
If you don't know
Just want to say to the brother cross the way,
thank you for being a friend,
See that cellphone camera recording, captured
the truth that would repeat over and over again.
Nobody will deny the struggle was real,
A chokehold, followed by a swarm of officers
while crying I can't breathe; you know the deal.
For the officers, this was just an effort to curtail
this major crime of state tax law,
But for millions across the country, my fight to
breathe is what they saw.
Took forever for a medical team to arrive,
Eleven times stating I can't breathe,
Yet the medics come just as disorganized,
Like they didn't know the tools to keep someone
alive.
Oh yeah, I'm just faking for my own health,
How about that oxygen and stretcher,
Can a brother get some help?
So because you thinking I'm faking, you feel first
for a pulse before retrieving any equipment.
You can't make this stuff up.
Police account and external examination are two
different things,
One claiming no visible injuries, the other
indicating the telltale signs of suffering.
Strap muscle hemorrhages in his neck and
petechial hemorrhages in his eyes,
Indicating there was more that happened than
the officers wanted the community to recognize.
If you don't know,
Now you know.
I can't breathe

I can't breathe
I can't breathe
I can't breathe
I can't breathe
I can't breathe
I can't breathe
I can't breathe
I can't breathe
I can't breathe
I can't breathe
I told you with my very last breath.
A hustling entrepreneur's life shrouded in death.

#ForEricGarner

My Block

This is my block,
This is my neighborhood,
This is where I do school, work, and play,
Where I mind my own business, go about my day.
Just left the market to pick up some cigarillos,
Reports will say they were stolen, and you know
how reporting goes.
Then an officer appears, shows up alone,
Yelling at us through his police vehicle window.
We were walking in the middle of street and here
begins the talk,
You want us to move to the sidewalk.
For what reason do I even have to stop and listen
to you?
You're on our block just visiting so don't tell me
what I have to do.
So I fit the description of a suspect,
Someone suspected of a convenience store theft.
I'm leaving the scene, crossing the street with
my friend,
You call the dispatcher, calling about two
black men.

The officer then uses his vehicle as security
To block us in traffic, and we're just crossing the
street.
So there's an altercation, an argument between
the officer and me,
Two shots fired from inside the vehicle, one
grazing the other missing, you see
I take off quick in a run

Officer pursues on foot, and what's the point?
I stop and turn towards the officers, hands up,
don't shoot.
A big black teen can only be seen as a threat, so
firing shots is what you proceed to do.
Can't you tell this is my block? We just go about
what we normally do,
It's not until something pops off that you ever see
the boys in blue.
You can't tie it with a bow and wrap the situation
pretty and neat,
For a body lying in a pool of blood for hours dead
in the streets.
After all the evidence and reports were presented
what did the jury decide?
A jury of three black and nine white, the outcome
was to not indict.
Waves of protests, looting and unrest span the
city night after night,
Will we ever see the scales of justice in balance
and just simply do what is right?
Will we just become numb to the matter of black
lives?

#ForMichaelBrownJr.

Sixteen

Born to a single mom and absentee father, he was
only seventeen.
Life was just really beginning, him planning to
pursue his future dreams.
Life wasn't easy, he had a tough ride:
Drugs and gang made up the violence living on
the West Side.
Although he had learning disabilities and had
been diagnosed with complex mental health
issues,
He wasn't going to let his past dictate his path
nor his future.
School suspensions, expulsions, truancies and
drug arrests,
Just life lessons along his road of life, but didn't
have to lead to death.
A night call was made to investigate a situation,
A guy was breaking into vehicles and carrying a
knife; this could be a dangerous confrontation.
Confronted by the police, he was asked to drop
the knife,
It wasn't a case of mistaken identity or an officer
fearing for his life.
McDonald was walking away when the officer
fired the first shot,
Within only fourteen to fifteen seconds, sixteen
shots was what McDonald got.
The officer was on the scene less than thirty
seconds before he opened fire,

Only six seconds from getting out of car, he began
shooting without it being required.
Sixteen
Sixteen
First shot fired, McDonald fell to the ground,
More shots, more shots, man down, man down.
Sixteen shots
And the first responder didn't see the need to
use force,
The other officers on that scene made weapons
their choice.
Sixteen
So what was your excuse?
Was it the thrill of the chase, that your authority
you decided to abuse?
Sixteen
Expending the bullet capacity of your 9mm
semiautomatic,
No plan for de-escalation or situation assessment
was your chosen tactic.
Sixteen
One police report said the officer feared he'd be
rushed with a knife,
While another report noted the knife was found
in closed position, and you were fearing for your
life?
Sixteen
Medical report concludes it was a death by
homicide,
Shots in the neck, chest, back, both arms, right
leg and a grazed wound on his scalp could not be
denied.
Sixteen
Dashcam from officers' cars with five videos
known to exist,

When the written reports conflict with the footage, you know something is up with this.
Investigations, withholding documents until a settlement with the family was reached,
Protests across the city extended more than days and went on for weeks and weeks.
This crazy code of silence by police, few are willing to break,
Like a jump rope rhyme ends, how many shots did he take?
One, two, three, four, five, six, seven, eight, nine, ten, eleven, twelve, thirteen, fourteen, fifteen, sixteen

#ForLaquanMcDonald

Just Another Bad Call

Just another bad call,
Like that child's game of telephone,
At what point did it get twisted and messed up?
"911. What's your emergency?" the operator
answers the call,
Report of a guy with a gun pointing at the
recreation center,
"Gun probably fake, just a juvenile" was what the
caller told the dispatcher.
Two cops and their trainees out on patrol sent to
investigate,
Evidently, they missed the message that this was
probably a child and the gun was likely fake.
So thinking they were dealing with a potential
active shooter,
Justifying not charging the officers who were
within feet of the twelve-year-old child with their
cruiser.
Total disregard for department policy,
Sound judgment went out of the window for black
with gun was what they did see.
Child reached into his waistband, pulling out his
toy gun.
Cops said they shouted warnings for him to drop
his firearm,
Nothing was done in the situation to de-escalate,
Just a boy lying in the snow-covered grass
without receiving first aid.
Somebody else showed up and provided medical
attention until the ambulance did arrive,

But for all their training, the officers wanted to do something but didn't know what to do, was their version, their side.

Kid's eyes rolling to the back of his head, barely breathing, no rescue squad and nothing you could have done?

Seriously, a trained officer couldn't radio for medical assistance or help of any kind? That's job one.

Worried about their administrative hearings when they didn't follow policy, no not at all.

But a twelve-year-old with a pellet gun lost his life, and to a family, he will not return just because of another bad call.

#ForTamirRice

Jury Duty

Ain't no sign up, mad rush or fast fury;
To be called to serve on jury duty.
The selection process almost functions like a
lottery,
You never know if you might be called or how
long the case might be.
It's the nature of the case and the judge that
makes the ultimate decision,
While seeing justice served is the community's
vision.
Given all the police brutality cases that have been
recently raised,
The pressure on a team of jurors becomes more
stressful as time slowly clicks away.
So before the jury is the case of Walter Scott,
Simple enough, the story begins with a routine
traffic stop.
Cop goes back to his car to run the license,
Scott bolts from the car and runs, which doesn't
make sense.
Doesn't take long before a foot chase ensues,
Video captures Scott being shot in the back, now
coming to conclusion is what the jury has to do.
Yes, it was foolish for Scott to jump the scene and
try to leave,
But there was no cause for this excessive use of
force that ended his life so tragically.
So he had warrants for unpaid child support,
Yet that's not the reason now we have both sides
in court.
How do we address the officer's accountability?

To charge with murder or manslaughter are the options given to the jury.
Sufficient provocation, imminent danger, forethought, and self-defense needed to be defined,
It's not like we've been given several days, we have a set amount of time.
After almost three hours of deliberation
This jury regretted to inform the court that they were unable to come to an unanimous decision.
A mistrial is declared, contributing to ongoing community tension.
While efforts to try the case again would call for everyone's patience,
Scott's family became an example of leadership and grace given the stressful circumstances.
Although the Scott family was awarded 6.5 million in a civil settlement,
It does nothing to justify the ongoing police brutality or bring Walter Scott's life back.

#ForWalterScott

Custody

Can I just be who I be,
Without being categorized as suspicious because
of the color you see?
It's just like some light switch that goes off in the
brain,
All you see is black, so doing your job is your
claim.
So you say I had an illegal switchblade, a knife;
On these B'more streets, I cannot protect my own
life?
Heck, truth be told these guys in blue never show
on our side of town,
These streets are more dangerous every day,
but you're trying to get recognition by pinning
another black man down.
I was arrested without force or incident,
Somebody took a video, so you can see how things
really went:
Two officers pin this black man to the ground,
And you don't call that force? I believe I hear the
crickets sound.
Screaming with hands cuffed behind my back,
Put in a tactical hold before placement in the van
as matter of fact.
Got loaded in like an animal faced down into the
old paddy wagon,
My safety was not considered, not seat-belted for
this situation.
Despite cries indicating that I couldn't breathe,
They ignored and kept on rolling towards the
station, as if I was a child not to be heard or seen.

Not until at the station we arrive,
Paramedics are requested and take me for that hospital ride.
Three broken vertebrae and injured voice box,
In a coma until the day of death, and the argument is to prosecute or not.
Being black, you're never the victim in such a case,
They'll dig up your history, any flaw in your past to justify their approach anyway.
So a little weed in the system had me screaming, acting like a goof,
Those four stops were not made for just my behavior, and even your own timeline shows the proof.
How much movement could there actually be?
Handcuffed face down with shackles on my feet.
So your report says all the injuries sustained,
That I'm the one at fault for the injuries I retained.
City continues to burn with riots and anger in full release,
'Cause why are we the only ones ending up dead in your custody?
Failure to ask the right questions to rightly pursue this,
Resulted in a black man dead and police officers acquitted.

#ForFreddieGray

Homeless

You really don't know the story, I had someplace
to go,
Worked on a farm for a couple of months while
living with a friend in San Diego.
Just stopped for a little adventure, to see what I
could see,
Maybe skateboard, get some sun, out here on
Venice Beach.
It was Cinco de Mayo, and I had something to
drink,
May cause me to wobble a little, but I wasn't on
the brink.
There's a local center where I can stop, grab some
food and a change of clothes,
So quick to label a person's situation without the
facts you should know.
But I'm homeless,
Yeah, homeless.
So you get a call from a somebody with a
complaint,
Claimed I'm harassing customers outside the
restaurant; not true, 'cause I ain't.
I had a little drink that had me for a brief minute
staggering,
And just maybe my speech was doing some
slurring.
I was not making some inappropriate public
display,
I just was getting where I was going, walking
away.

But like most police reports around here go on and on,
I had walked off toward the bar and started yelling at patrons.
I started to push the bouncer,
And the police appear magically,
Said I refused to follow orders and turn around,
This when it turns into a full fight with flailing arms until taken to the ground.
So they call me homeless,
Yeah, homeless.
My account, police account,
Videotape evidence will soon lead to settlement amount.
So I'm the one who must have been on something strong,
But reaching for your partner's holster is where you got it wrong.
Tunnel vision? Please, you were on that authority high,
You pulled the trigger that day and decided I was to die.
Had a three-year old son and a family,
Just came out to the west-coast to look for better opportunities.
Another life lost, and the police try to apologize for their mess,
Justify the use of deadly force on a man they labeled homeless.

#ForBrendonGlenn

Same Name

Same color,
Same gender,
Same first and last name,
Same general geographic zone,
Broken taillight is why you came.
You issue the ticket to the driver to send them on their way,
But hold up the passenger, Darrius Stewart, has warrants, let's see what the records say.
So to the back of the police car, you place the teen until you get verification,
Investigators give their point of view for the situation.
The officer tried to open the door to handcuff a nineteen-year-old Stewart, who kicked the door and went into a mode of attack.
He was tired of being accused of the same old thing, he'd already been stopped before, months back.
By now, should they have not had the technology to locate, pull up name, date of birth?
You can't access pictures or info from other agencies, and so my life is what it's worth?
Investigators say that Stewart had grabbed the officer's handcuffs and swung,
Rather than explain, try to de-escalate the situation, or to stun,
The officer shot the teen with a gun.
Now here at the regional medical center in critical condition,

A life on the verge of death because of same name recognition.
Not able to really access records, verify and guarantee
That this was the guy they were truly after with all certainty,
He had been stopped before, for the same thing,
Somebody with a series of warrants that had the same name.
Yet a misunderstanding turned deadly, as the investigation goes,
He could've been a doctor headed to the university.
Another young man of color who will never realize that dream,
Still no answers and no one will take blame;
For death of someone with the exact same name.

#ForDarriusStewart

Campus Police

As a new student on campus, you take the tour
to familiarize yourself with everything you need:
The library, the cafeteria, your dorm and the
bookstore, oh yeah, the campus police.
You go to the library to submerge yourself in the
words of many books,
To write research papers for professors who over
their bifocals give you questioning looks.
In the cafeteria, it's not just about the food;
It's meeting and hanging out with your friends,
just having a time that's good.
The dorm is the place where you reside and rest
your head at night,
Where you get calls from your mom at least once
a week to make sure everything is alright.
It's off to the bookstore to be sure you get your
school spirit style,
Sweatshirts, jackets, pompoms and backpacks
and other mascot driven supplies.
You've taken a tour of the campus and you've
learned your way around,
Then you learn about the campus police just in
case of trouble you should be found.
Well, on this night, it was really late,
Campus police pulls a guy over for failure to
display a front license plate.
In the initial police report, the officer said he was
forced to shoot the driver because he was being
dragged,
The car was nearly about to run him over,
different story from the body cam he had.

The released video shows the driver to be turning on the ignition,
The cop tells the driver to take off his seatbelt while he reaches for the driver's door,
Yells, stops, then draws his gun and thrust the gun right through the open car window.
A single round shooting the driver in the head,
This driver wasn't wanted for murder; there was no reason for him to end up dead.
Criminal charges were brought and filed,
Prosecution and defense rest their cases at the trial.
Fate now lies in the hands of a jury for decision,
To see if this campus police officer will end up with a conviction.

#ForSamuelDubose

The Beat

Fall into the rhythm every time,
Never miss a step; keeping the time.
Bass drum, snare drum, hi-hat, hi-hat,
Early basic pattern you learn in your first tap.
Snare drum, bass drum, snare drum, bass drum,
hi-hat,
You feel the rhythm from your head to toe, yes,
this is where I want to be at.
Just leaving a gig, driving down I-95,
Bum car got me stranded, but I'm not leaving it
with my main set inside.
Yeah, friend with an SUV offered to help,
Not enough space to satisfy myself.
Roadside assistance called from AT&T,
Just have to sit and wait until they come
rescue me.
Unmarked car comes and parks,
Thought it could have been some form of help
until this discussion starts.
Plainclothes officer steps out of the car in the
open,
Doesn't realize that the phone, his words, and
actions are recording.
In my head and in my hands, I just play to the
beat,

Feel the rhythm in my soul at points forgetting to even breathe.

Bass drum, snare drum, and Hi-hat, hi-hat,
Snare drum, bass drum, one, two, three, four
Pulse racing, heart racing, God don't let it be.
Not trying to become the next hashtag, can't this dude just leave?
But like many others, the story unfolds,
Can't expect the outcome to be different, truth untold.
The officer claims fear of life, pointing a max laser with guide light on the gun,
The situation so crazy, wish that roadside assistance would hurry and come.
My body's found two hundred feet from my car and a chrome, .380 handgun about seventy feet from my car, so explain that one. Shot in the heart and the lungs,
This officer, unidentified officer, just continues his lie and lets it linger on,
Those who now watch this case await on pins and needles:
Hoping, praying, that the truth will finally yield a conviction.
Hi-hat right hand, snare drum left hand,
Bass drum right foot, one, two, three, four.
Mind inside the rhythm of early learned basic beat,
The ones that rock the party, the ones that move your feet.
Yes, yes, y'all
Yes, yes, y'all
To the beat
To the beat

#ForCoreyJones

Music Hustle

Everybody got something,
A little something on the side;
To help with the incidentals,
Just in case of emergency money in a jar to hide.
So you can say that music is my thing,
Out in front of the store or in the barber shop;
Not out here for a record deal trying to sing.
Just trying to keep those bills paid.
Hustle on music hustling,
Got your CDs here,
Got your CDs here,
I've got you covered, don't have no fear.
Rap, Jazz, a little R&B,
If you need your music, you get the best from me,
I do what I do to get my hustle on.
Not always safe in these streets, gotta pack a gun.
Pretty good day, things going right,
Nothing could prepare me for the fatal events of
the night.
So because one doesn't follow an officer's order
and immediately comply,
It justifies a struggle, putting a gun to my head
to die.
CNN reports that no federal charges to be filed
by state investigation,
Regardless of the deadly end of the situation,
protests were revived across the nation.
Whether you bought a CD or not,
I didn't deserve the bullet, the death I got.
Just trying to keep the bills paid, music hustling.

#ForAltonSterling

Acquitted

Give me an A, you've got your A, you've got your A
Give me a C, you've got your C, you've got your C
Give me a Q, you've got your Q, you've got your Q
Video live streamed showed to the world enough
proof.
Give me an U, you've got your U, you've got your U
Give me an I, you've got your I, you've got your I
Give me a T, you've got your T, you've got your T
Give me a T, you've got your T, you've got your T
Give me an E, you've got your E, you've got your E
Give me a D, you've got your D, you've got your D
He already said he had a gun and was reaching
for his ID,
Second-degree manslaughter and prosecuted to
the full extent of the law it should be.
Shot, murdered in front of his girlfriend and
young child,
Blood spattered everywhere, but the jury's
deliberation only took a little while.
Pulled him over for a broken taillight,
Yeah, doing your job, yeah right.
But being quick, seeing a black man with a right
to carry his gun, you assume
That your life was endangered and you were in
impending doom.
Give me an E, you've got your E, you've got your E
Now with bated breath, all wait to see what the
verdict will be,
Will a committed school cafeteria worker's life
be valued, or will another cop get off scot-free?
Give me a D, you've got your D, you've got your D

Before the gavel slams, we know what the verdict is going to be,
Images of the live stream of cries and blood-spattered,
Ever etched in our memory as courts continue to say black lives don't matter.
Can't get the decency of an American citizen,
More racial tension across the nation now more than it's ever been.
Even murder in front of a woman and child should have violated some policy,
But no, when the judgment came down, cop acquitted, not guilty.
ACQUITTED?
ACQUITTED?
HE WAS ACQUITTED?
ACQUITTED!
ACQUITTED.

#ForPhilandoCastille

If You Missed It

Did you hear it on the radio?
Did you see it on tv?
Did the story make the paper?
On social media did you see?
Facebook, Twitter, Instagram?
Maybe you caught it on the live stream?
But before the ones that got all over media attention,
This one slipped through with only a few mentions.
Behavior technician at a group home just doing his day's work,
Ran out the house after an autistic client to prevent him from in the street being hurt.
His client had a toy truck, but neighbors thought and reported it as a gun,
The technician with his hands raised shouts out to make cops aware of the situation.
"It's a toy, it's only a toy!" the tech shouted with his hands raised,
The officer fired a shot at the unarmed worker, not even phased.
So are you getting all this?
This story is too unbelievable for you to miss.
Worker was just trying to keep his autistic client calm,
Shot was fired in the worker's leg; it was a toy truck not a firearm.
It's amazing how the stories change,
'Cause once evidence is produced into play, what more can you say?

Someone's cell phone footage caught the exchange,
The aftermath of officers conflicting stories couldn't be erased
Sufficient coverage recorded, offered as part of the case.
So what more did you miss? I'm just sharing what the reports say:
An initial charge of one felony count of attempted manslaughter and a misdemeanor count of negligence that day.
But during a later hearing, the charges changed
Two felony counts of attempted manslaughter, but on pins and needles the community remains.
But in a city already plagued by issues with infighting and crooked cops,
Wouldn't be the least surprised if the charges don't stick and the officer gets off.
So if you didn't catch it on the radio,
If you didn't catch it on the news,
If you didn't catch in the paper,
Or on social media, you didn't view,
The story still bears telling,
No matter what, you'll find it to be true:
Even having your hands raised, they won't believe you.

#ForCharlesKinsey

Redemption

Redemption is, people at one time not considered
a people, staking their claim,
Coming to their rightful inheritance and
reclaiming their identity and name.

Redemption is, crushing every stereotype,
Not to be put in a box, just want to be judged
according to what's right.

Redemption is, one hope, one faith one family
Willing to do the work of justice and equality.

Redemption is respecting me, my body, the skin
I'm in.
Don't allow fear to block the blessing as I extend
to you my hand.

Redemption is attending public meetings and
community town halls,
Putting forth the hard questions to leaders for
the benefit of all.

Redemption goes beyond just marches and
speeches for a cause.
It's getting to the polls, voting people out and in,
changing laws.

Redemption is brothers and sisters being able to
hang out, fellowship, have friends over,
Not fearing driving while black at night for those
without cause to pull you over.

Redemption is being proud of who I am and the ability to express it the way I please,
And if you can't get with that expression just keep it moving, please.

Redemption is stretched out on the altar, kneeling on the floor,
Seeking God for answers and asking Him, "How much more?"

Redemption is accepting and acknowledging that you have the right to exist,
Just 'cause your experience differs doesn't mean that my voice you dismiss.

Redemption is getting reparations due,
Not everybody got their forty acres and a mule.

Redemption is honor, respect, truth, faith, and love;
Grace given, grace received, and a hope for better days.

Redemption is knowing and walking in the fact that I'm free, indeed;
Never a solitary soul can take that freedom from me.

One day it will come
Someday it will come
And I will tell them
I will tell them all
What redemption is

Just Us

BUT LET JUSTICE RUN DOWN LIKE WATER,
AND RIGHTEOUSNESS LIKE
A MIGHTY STREAM.

AMOS 5:24 (NKJV)

On the Banks

On the banks, I stood, had wandered off to play,
It was as normal a hot and humid day.
I saw these ships come sailing in,
Men of different shapes and sizes, with pale
white skin.
With one shouting orders as they began to
descend,
With weapons in hand could only mean ill intent.
They did not come in peace or in goods to trade,
They were looking for bodies to take to their land;
the making of a slave.
Many small villages they manage to pillage,
Capturing the strongest of the men, women, and
children.
The screams and cries of elders could be heard
for miles around,
The message of the white man's terror attacks
messaged with each drumbeat's sound.
By the time I got close enough to my home to see,
My village had been burned to the ground, only
thing left are my memories.
Scared for my life but don't know what to do,
Return to the banks, but find I'm not alone—
others had the same idea too.
We watched from afar, covered in the darkness,
Not understanding the great terror of this
madness.
That those taken would be gone far away,
Never to return, Never to return to their homeland
or shores' banks.
Just a child filled with curiosity,

I had followed a small animal in the opposite direction of my family.

I wandered off and missed being captured, yet should I give thanks?

Not knowing if my family is on the ship that's launching off from the banks.

Tonight my prayers I utter in silence looking at the stars,

Praying for each and every soul, wherever they are.

Some may be chained or jumping overboard they might be,

Let their eternal souls find safety.

Somehow I'll manage to live off the land,

Remember the lessons taught, work with the strength of my own hands.

I must continue to watch and pray,

Just never know if terror will return to these banks.

Middle Passage

In the middle of the ocean
In the middle of seas
Storms are raging
Winds are blowing
A ship full of black bodies

Men, women, children
Families divided, no home, no land
Bound and chained to each other, tight
Like sardines in a can

Lying in their own urine and feces with no place to go
Some daring to jump overboard, for in
death they'd free their souls
Human cargo trafficking, nothing more than property
Fed slop like animals, no care for their well-being

Prayers and songs uttered in tongues unknown
Just longing to survive the day and anything to get back home
But when land the ship finally did see
Unloaded like cattle and welcomed to a new world of slavery

Auction Block

Families are broken and separated;
time keeps moving like a clock
To be poked and pulled, every crevice
examined on the auctioning block
A bidding war begins, like prized cattle each body is raised
Men, women, boys, and girls; the very
young and those of great age

To the block, a young woman stood with
child feeding on her breast
They roughly removed the child from her
as her own milk ran down her chest
Fertile young woman, they announced
and then began the bidding war
I'll offer twelve bits for the child and a
half bit for the child she bore

Young man of no more than twenty years
Beautiful, like Michelangelo's *David* with cocoa dark skin
Examined eyes, pulled hair and then looked at his teeth
Looked at the build of his arms and legs,
examination not yet complete
Then the unthinkable occurred to add to his suffering
They grabbed his male privates, auctioneer
announcing he would be good for breeding

From the rising of the sun until it sets indicating the day's end
Men haggling over prices of humans
again and again and again
Then, once purchased and the buyer receives the bill of sale
You hear the pain and agony of burning flesh,
as with each brand results in a yell

No country, no home, no family
No rights, your own name
No language, no culture no religious practices
That you can express or claim

You survive the luxury cruise ship ride
Malnourished, poor conditions but still survived
To remind you that you ain't free no more
To be placed on the auction block, don't stop, move forward

Plantation

People with purpose for their lives

Lives separated from children and wives

Another's land, another's space

No voice of your own, got to know your place

To work for free from dusk to dawn

And eat the scraps barely enough to survive on

The cries of rape and whippings heard across
slave quarters

Intending to make examples of those who'd try
to escape fenced borders

Oh that one day we'd all be free

No more chains binding Negro, Colored, Black,
Afro-American, African American humanity

On the Run

Run, Nigger, run
Through the woods
Through creek beds
Hiding in wood piles
Behind empty sheds
If tracks are picked up, won't make it far
Will end up beaten or hanged or back to the start

Run, Nigger, run
Dogs panting
Horse hooves beating
Signs posted
They looking for
Hunting for
Searching for me

Run, Nigger, run
Staying close to the water
So the dogs will lose the scent
Seconds to minutes, minutes to hours
Not sure where all the time went
Tired, hungry, scrounging for food
Can't get sick now
That would be no good

Run nigger run
They figure I've got no place to hide
Didn't count on safe houses and following a star
as a guide
Sores and blisters on tired weary feet
Just got to keep running on
Just one more day, and I'll be free

Dred Scott

Five of nine justices would make a decision.
Determine the value of my life—their mission.
Question of the time, if my owner traveling with me,
What would I be considered once residing in a free territory?
The argument of popular sovereignty was the debated issue,
State's rights as applied to slavery would cause much violence to ensue.
The Supreme Court would go with the majority:
A slave would not be free based on his residence, whether or not in free territory.
At the time the constitution was drafted, blacks were nowhere in mind
They were merely seen as property, not to be citizens at any time.
For those who initially read or will read this, see or saw,
Property could not be taken from a person without due process of law.
Tension over this and regional decisions would continue to burn like never before,
Burning for another four years until exploding into civil war.

Abolition

Years before the Civil War made the pages of
history,
A movement using risky and radical tactics whose
focus was anti-slavery,
To put an end to a practice with a goal of
immediate emancipation,
To put end to discrimination and segregation.
These people were different from their slave-
owning others, who thought emancipation should
gradually come to be,
Or those who sought just to restrict slavery to
existing areas and prevent its spread to further
Western territories.
Nothing like a great revival to get a man's heart
stirred,
Second Great Awakening fueled the religious
fervor of the cause through the word.
Many became prompted to advocate for
emancipation on religious grounds,
These abolitionist ideas in northern churches
and politics were most likely to be found.
These ideas created animosity and division
between regions north and south,
Then came violent mobs and a gag rule banning
antislavery consideration from anyone's mouth.
From literature and speeches and conventions
the momentum was building, and well,
Until abolitionists began to dispute largely among
themselves.
Black, white, men, and women on the process of
how to work this through,

Soon efforts were overshadowed by secession crisis, slave revolts, and yeah, that civil war thing too.

With the passage of the Thirteenth Amendment, the abolition society to many was no longer necessary,

But the need for land, the vote, and education made it still relevant, quite the contrary.

Leadership continued the work the abolitionists had begun,

Yet the society no longer exists, the quest for equality still lives on.

War

Wasting
Another's
Resources

Warring
Against
Rights

Wrong
About
Race

Wins
Achieve Abolition and
Reconstruction

Work
Affords
Resolution

Not on the Record

Not a cattle thief or bank robbery in territories
out west
For alleged crimes lynching was the punishment
the south liked best
You just simply had to be accused of a crime
Round up a bunch of the boys with a meeting
place and time
No judge or jury here to distinguish the truth
from lie
We're just taking the law into our own hands and
at the end, somebody is going to die
This form of punishment and intimidation
became a tactic of terror
For putting blacks in their place, and not all cases
made the record

Following the Civil War and the close of
reconstruction Southern whites were determined
to end Northern and black participation
They didn't want Blacks and Yankees meddling
in their affairs
But for the civil rights of Black Americans at that
point, the Northerners didn't even care
So here at this intersection of White harmony
Came an era of laws to affirm White superiority
No longer would there be constitutional protections
States governments respond to the issue of race
with their own directions
With Jim Crow, Blacks are barred from voting,
public office, and jury service
Officials felt no obligation to argue or protest this

So White mobs would rise and supremacy groups
would grow and flourish
Night raids, burning fields, dragging men from
their beds
People come from miles around hearing of the
entertainment ahead
Sometimes it would begin by chaining or hanging
a body to a tree
Followed by burning flesh for all the good citizens
to see
Sometimes they would beat and stomp the victim
until unrecognized
Hurling insults and derogatory names to strip the
victim of their pride
Maybe you just own a business that made you
competition
Let's accuse you of a crime and get a mob in on
the action

More than four thousand blacks were lynched
across twenty states
Between 1877 and 1950 is what the records say
A lynching became like a community party
Whites watched and participated in the black
victims torturing
Mutilation, dismemberment, and burning at the
stake
These lynchings would then appear on postcards
that you could buy from the drugstore and take

You could be lynched if they thought you were
treating them with less respect
Or for non-criminal violations of social customs,
you weren't to forget
Lynchings based on fear of interracial sex

Black on White sexual violence had become a
widespread myth
For telling the truth of consensual interracial
interactions journalist Ida B. Wells received her
own lynching threats
Lynchings based on some social transgression
Because I bumped into you or didn't step down
from the sidewalk so to burn is the lesson
Lynchings just on allegations of a crime
Even testifying against someone White, you could
be lynched in just a matter of time
Didn't matter how much you said or proof showed
you were innocent
If you were Black being accused by a White
anything you said was easily dismissed
Lynchings even became social events publicized
in the local paper
Just shows the lack of human decency; moral
deprivation

No justice for the victim or legal repercussions
to be found
Yet the blood of those lynched, record no record,
cries to us from the ground

Emancipation

Announcement
Announcement for your hearing,
Announcement
Announcement for your viewing,
Announcement calling for verification of receipt.

Announcement for immediate release,
Announcement
Announcement for immediate action,
Announcement
Preliminary announcement, a warning that in all
states yet in rebellion would declare their slaves
from this point forward and forever free.
Announcement
That was only a preliminary, issued following the
Union victory at the Battle of Antietam.
Announcement
This is a commitment of the government and its
armed forces today,
To liberate the slaves in rebel states.
This the government proudly proclaims,
Emancipation, freedom has come, it says.
Announcement
Yet the border slave states and Confederate states
controlled by the Union army would be exempt
To a plan of gradual emancipation with
compensation, from the government they would
not consent.
Announcement
With such refusal, the stakes were extremely
high,

For the proclamation had no constitutional validity, the politicians recognized.
Announcement
A new birth of freedom, President Lincoln stated in his Gettysburg address,
By ratification of the Thirteenth Amendment, slavery could and would be abolished.
Announcement
Neither slavery nor voluntary servitude,
None of this throughout the United States would continue.
Announcement
You have heard the reading of the announcements,
Please govern yourselves accordingly.

Reconstruction

To build again
To build up
To reorganize
Reconstruct
Nearly four million slaves gained freedom
To the South, it was a devastating loss
So to control labor and behavior of former slaves,
they passed restrictive "Black Codes"

To build again
To build up
To reorganize
Reconstruct
Outrage over the codes caused a great divide
A radical reconstruction would soon turn the tide

To build again
To build up
To reorganize
Reconstruct
Newly enfranchised Blacks gained voice
They finally had a chance to speak and exercise
their rights as meant
Winning elections in state legislature and even
Congress

To build again
To build up
To reorganize
Reconstruct
But reactionary forces like the Ku Klux Klan

Were by no means going to stand for that
So in less than a decade changes of radical
reconstruction would be reversed
Violence would restore white supremacy in the
South as it was first

To build again
To build up
To reorganize
To reconstruct

Jim Crow

A derogatory name from a minstrel act,
A hit among white audiences, the actor painted
his face black.
Jokes and songs promoting slave stereotypes for
mere entertainment,
Turned to laws to black freedom's detriment.
Restriction to voting rights,
Restriction, voting only to those whose
grandfather had held the right,
Restriction, a ban on interracial relationships,
Restrictions, weren't none on that middle passage
ship.
Restriction, clauses allowing businesses to
separate their black and white customers,
Restriction, none from preventing me a job being
your personal driver for your car or cleaning your
dirty home.
Then comes the *Plessy v. Ferguson* Supreme
Court decision impacting all near and far,
Louisiana would now have the right to require
Blacks to ride in different railroad cars.
The result of this decision became so widespread,
Now called separate but equal, philosophy upheld
Adoption of segregated restaurants,
Adoption of segregated public bathrooms,
Adoption of segregated water fountains,
Adoption of segregated other facilities,
Jim Crow, a joke then law meant to divide

Would find its end with *Brown vs. Board of
Education,* the Supreme Court would again decide.
Jump, Jump, Jim Crow
Jump, Jump, Jim Crow
You will never be revived, this for sure we know.

Equal To

Equal to
    Same as
    Not same, nor completely different
    Not superior, or inferior
    Not added to, nor subtracted from
    Not greater or less than
    Not multiplied or divided

Equal to
    In capacity
    In ability
    In concept
    In design
    In body
    In spirit
    In soul
    In mind

Equal to
    Given access
    Given time
    Given opportunity
    Given education
    Given the rights owed to me
    Given my citizenship in this country

Equal to

Equality
> Not based on city, state or regional location
> Not based on economic status or occupation
> Not based on level or where you get your education
> By reason of birth as a citizen of this great nation

Equal to

To the Back

At the front of the bus, I pay my fare,
Then step down to go back out to enter in the rear.
So many seats in front there be,
Yet to the back we go, if you are black like me.

At a restaurant, I can cook, clean and take orders as you would,
But to the back, I must go to purchase my own food.

For even entertainment, just going to a picture show,
Paying my ticket, taking the stairs on the side to the balcony entrance in the back I have to go.

Tired of second-hand books,
second-hand scraps, while you get the best to eat.
Tired of sharecropping, doing the works with shotgun housing in the field,
You take the best for yourselves,
Cheating financially, what a raw deal.

Planning, meeting to organize
Boycotts to demand our civil rights.
No longer will we as citizens be treated as second class,
I've earned a seat at the table,
I will no longer take the seat in the back.

To the back, I am not destined,
To the back is not to be my position,
To the back, I will no longer go,
Just because you want it to be so.
You may see yourself as superior,
But that does not make me inferior.

Born here
Live here
Work here
School here
Family here
Home here
Citizen here

The back is not to be,
In the front is where you will see me.

Letter from the Clergy of Color

Dear Clergy,

Something from my heart I want to share,
As locked up over a cause I hold dear.
Like Paul, we are in bonds to see a people free,
Yet the actions of myself and others you declare
as unwise and untimely.

How can we claim to love a God we cannot see,
Yet treat his Negro children violently?
How can random lynching, entertainment if you
will,
Be justified in your eyes when the commandment
says, Thou shall not kill?

When Scripture says we are all members of the
body,
To exclude me from that image on the basis of
color is somewhat bias.

If Jesus loves all the children of the world,
Does he stop when they become full grown?
Or does his love expire because of your exegetical
say so?

If I'm a hand, am I not a part of the body?
If I'm a foot, am I not a part of the body?
Does one part of the body discontinue its use?
Does it not continue its function because some
quarrel between parts ensues?

So what do we do? Recognize we are many but one,
Each contributing to the function of the whole to get the necessary job done.
Your contribution is no more or less important than mine,
Yet this work of justice demands our attention for it is way overdue, past time.
We are so hasty to rush in for knowledge and understanding we do not lack,
Does injustice exist here? We question and gather the facts.
Then on the basis of that information, we then seek to negotiate,
For the urgent need of brothers and sisters in this community is why we can no longer wait.
Then we must evaluate ourselves, self-purification,
Reflecting on maintaining integrity and non-violence in the face of such humiliation.
When we see according to Augustine "An unjust law is no law at all,"
We recognize the time for direct action, and with faith we must stand tall.

Yet peaceful protest you say must be condemned,
But unjust violent actions by others you fail to mention.
To understand the frustrations of those of color, you will not even try.
You turn your head in denial, as by your silence you assert our cause to be a lie.
That I have to distinguish the just versus the unjust seems somewhat insane,

As clergy we are commissioned to teach the truth and complexities of the word, not just the simple or the mundane.

Do you not see bravery in the face of oppression?
Those humiliated yet maintaining integrity?
Are the dogs and water hoses targeting youth just a figment of imagination?
To be taunted, disrespected and called out of your name what you would call Christian?
Can we preserve the evil of segregation?
Where is your concern, your righteous indignation?
And you wonder why the church, young people no longer trust,
The world is changing around them, and without a word from you, they feel frustration, disgust.

As we look at the days ahead to continue to fight for what is right,
We continue with love in hearts and grace that endures with God's arm of protection through the night.
For those who are of the oppressed, yet long to be free, and they cannot wait forever.
When part of the body hurts, the whole body feels the pain,
For we are all in this together.

I will close with the words of the Apostle Paul, written in Ephesians 4:3, "Endeavouring to keep the unity of the Spirit in the bond of peace."

This we will continually do. I would hope that you would give voice and prayer to our call. I will yet pray for you.

For the love of Christ and the case of peace,

The clergy of color

The March

Buses arrive from across the nation,
In front of the monument, Lincoln, called the
great emancipator;
To acknowledge the equality of all mankind,
To march arm in arm and hand in hand, praying
our efforts would be realized.
An end to segregation and an unjust society,
No more back of the buses or stepping off the
sidewalk into the street.
I've contributed to the making of this country,
as did you,
My rights as a citizen are long overdue.
With signs, songs, prayers, and speeches,
Our commitment strengthens us for the journey.
We heard about America's check, returned for
insufficient funds.
Moved with resolve of the dream Dr. King shared
on that great national mall,
It's been a long road from boycotts of buses
To meetings and sit-ins and nonviolent protests.
We have come to this moment; people of all
colors, nations, and creeds, gathered here
To voice a call for unity, for equality, and justice
for all must be made truthfully clear.
Old and young,
Rich and poor,
White and black,
Protestant and Catholic,
Boys and girls,
Men and women
Filled the lawn that day,

To inform the nation of the work needed, and
that we have a say.
When the day is done, and the grounds return as
they were once more,
This day will live in history as the cause of justice
is worth fighting for.

A Shame

I don't know the deal with today's Negroes,
Caught up with fast money, sex, and clothes.
Out on the street corners selling drugs,
Me trying to flashback and remember the way
it was.
Being outside playing double dutch,
Fire hydrants blasting in the summer and such.
Playing spin the bottle when parents weren't
home,
Giggling with my girlfriends on the phone.
Saturdays in the shop getting hair pressed,
And dressing up for church in our Sunday best.
When spanking wasn't considered child abuse,
When preachers got up and actually told the
truth.
When it wasn't about you and not about me,
People came together as a community.
Parents are getting younger and younger,
Kids on medication so they can stay in their seats
longer,
Babies' mama or babies' daddies,
Messed up families ain't nobody happy.
Don't even talk about the mess in the church,
You can't find peace there for what it's worth.
I mean a body gets tired of being alone,
Shouldn't have to be scared to leave my own
home.
No hand raised in the black power fist,
The community has taken a whole different twist.
Neighbors don't know each other's names,
Drive-by shootings are just a game.

Black males going to jail not a big deal,
Politicians fighting and telling lies,
While our race and culture dies.
No more welfare, a Republican reaction,
Just like California and other states getting rid of
Affirmative Action.
Talking reparations, they need to hold to that
fight,
'Cause government could easily rescind the '64
Voting Rights.
People go way out to shop, buy a new coat,
Can't even beg a nigger to get out and vote.
Then be the first ones to complain,
When they have no right to mention the same.
Black colleges and businesses closing down,
Lack of support from the people for which they
were found.

Black folks splittin' further and further apart,
Get a little bit of cash flow; think we smart.
Like racism is over when ain't a thing changed,
Just more subtle now, and it's a shame.
A shame that we're blinded, that we cannot see
The hurt of our own people in poverty.
A shame we complain about our kids' education,
But will cuss out the teacher without hearing the
entire situation.
A shame when we make our voices heard after
the fact,
Then get mad about the decision when we were
the ones lax.
A shame how we manage to cut each other down,
Never coming together on any common ground.
A shame that it has to be that way,
Never seen nothing like it in all my days.

The Talk

They talk about the birds and the bees,
They talk about flowers and trees.
They talk about having a big sweet 16,
They talk about getting the car of their dreams.
They talk about love and marriage,
Bridal showers before baby carriage.
They talk about going to college and where they
will intern,
Then after that the home they'll buy and the
money they'll earn.
This is not the kind of conversation that
generations passed down to me,
Coming off the slave ships into a life of pain and
mystery.
The talk has always been about how to survive,
All that one could think of to just keep one alive.
So we followed the drinking gourd and relied on
the north star,
Connected to underground pathways, as the road
to freedom was far.
Given code words to listen for to let us know who
to trust,
Paying attention to signs and symbols to know
with whom we could talk.
From scratch we had to form everything on
our own,
Our original language, religion, culture stripped
to build this new land unknown.
Mind your manners, say "yes, sir," "no, sir," and
no extra comments,

Don't draw attention to yourself or make direct
eye contact.
If some wrongdoing you are ever accused,
A plan of safety will have to be made for your
rescue.
Because if they're in the wrong you'll never be
seen as right,
They'll come on their horses and burning crosses
to take you away in the night.
Look how far we've come since the days of
Reconstruction,
Building our own churches, schools, and
establishing community organizations.
Make the best of every opportunity, because it
surely ain't free,
They may only come around once when you're a
Negro like you and me.
We talk about rules and survival, about a people's
history,
The resilience and the knowing that even today
freedom is never really free.
We talk about the lynchings and the rape of Black
bodies,
They say time heals all wounds, but that doesn't
account for the internal, the things that you
don't see.
Got to be two times as good to get half as far,
This truth hasn't changed, no matter how
progressive we think we are.
Be aware of your environment, every movement,
every sound,
Eyes are watching your every move, looking for
an excuse to bring you down.
We talk about the marches, the protest of being
Black and proud,

About sitting at the back of buses, paying the same fare to ride across town.
We talk about the history of segregation,
Modern-day lynchings, and the rise of gentrification,
We talk about civil rights, voting rights and affirmative action,
We talk religion and politics and the continued search for satisfaction.
We talk about the importance of graduation,
and continuing forward to get your education.
We talk about using your gifts and allowing them to make room,
Think big, dream big, be your own boss, and entrepreneurs.
We talk about the ancestors, their blood still cries from the ground,
We talk discovering and searching our histories, weaving our voices to resound.
The talk has always been layered with issues, complexities,
Not always being able to say what we want to say or be what we want to be.
The struggle to do more than get by,
To mask our tears and hide our pain when we want to cry.
See, this first talk is like a loaded gun,
It's history and identity all wrapped up in one:
To tell you what they won't tell you, the authentic truth,
The beauty and value of who you are, just you.

Small Talk

Loud talk
Quiet talk
Angry talk
Joyful talk
Talk from ear to ear
Talking, sharing laughter, sharing fears.
School talk
First date talk
How-to-deal-with-police talk
Rape talk
Campus talk
Don't be a victim be a victor, domestic violence
talk.
Church talk
Testimony talk
Prayer at the altar talk
I talk
You talk
Us talk
We talk
Love talk
Marriage talk
Baby talk
Text talk
Face-to-face talk
Online talk
Coffee talk
Club talk
Bar talk
Slow wind on the dance floor talk
Street talk

Gospel talk
Blues talk
Jazz and R&B talk
Hip-hop talk
Music history debate talk
Barbershop talk
Salon talk
Getting-hair-done-coming-out-fierce talk.
Drunk talk
Weed talk
Floating over adversity talk
News talk
Politics talk
What's the bottom line talk
Grassroots talk
Organize talk
Let's bring together the fighting sides talk
Marching talk
Protesting talk
Walk and talk
Teacher talk
Student talk
Exchange of ideas talk
I talk
You talk
He talks
She talks
We talk
You talk
They talk
But at the end of the day, we talk
At the end of the day, we talk
Always talk
Sometimes talk
Often talk

At the end of the day
Bottom line, anytime
At the end of the day, we talk
We talk
We talk
Talk

Monica Leak

Just Us No Justice

Just I
Just You
Just He
Just She
Just We
Just They
Just Me
Just you
Just him
Just her
Just us
Just them
Just us

Just us, most frequently stopped and frisked.
Just us, followed through stores as if we're going
to shoplift.
Just us, a group of friends can't walk down the
street.
Just us, to be called thugs and hoodlums when
we're just trying to be.
Just us, sagging jeans and natural hairstyles,
Copying us but you wouldn't want to walk a mile
in our shoes, our shoes, our shoes.
You wouldn't want to walk a mile in our shoes,
our shoes, our shoes.

Just us, driving in our neighborhood, to get
stopped and pulled over.
Just us, to be pulled out of cars until they've
searched the whole vehicle over.

Just us, that even having a pool party with friends,
You find a reason to crash and begin your brand of law enforcement.

Just us, rushed and referred to special ed.
Why don't you challenge and teach like your certificate says?
Just us, you rezone, redistrict and redraw the lines.
Not wanting too many in your home or school zone, which is where the truth lies.
Just us, for the simplest offense, referred to the principal for the behavior,
Wanting suspension to be your savior.

Just us, when arrested require the use of excessive force,
But others stop for burgers and fries on the way to the jail, of course.
Just us, that don't live to tell the story of having to stand our ground,
When a tea and bag of Skittles are what is found.

Just us, that because we know our rights and articulate them you call it disrespect,
But the next day you can find us dead in a cell, call it suicide, and that ain't suspect?
Just us reaching for license and registration and still get shot,
No charges filed, no punishment for the cop?

Just us, it's all fine when we're playing, taking hits on the field,
But you can take offense because instead of stand we kneel?
Just us, that you can justify
Redrawing voting districts and changing voting days and times,
All in the name of reforming suspected voter fraud,
When it's you that needs investigating, who do you think you are, God?

Just us, that upset you when we have our own, BET, TVONE, and sitcoms, movies, music, and shows.
We're fine as long as we're shucking it up and entertaining you, but if we do it for ourselves, you say we're being racists too?

Just us, when you label us very articulate,
Maybe that's because of colleges and universities to which we went.
Maybe for all your knowledge based on stereotype, Not every Black person is living that thug and ghetto life.

Just us, living in the lap of poverty,
Like nobody sees the trailer parks or the broken down trucks behind the trees.
Just us, living on the welfare,
Check the statistics because others rates are higher.

See this what happens when you go off assumption and rumor?
You play into a stereotype and fail to get the truth you searched for.

Just us, that you tell to get over the past.
Just us, that you tell that we live in a post-racial time, well that sure didn't last.
Even with a man in office, many of our community issues did not get to the floor,
For those in power made sure to knock everything he offered through the door.

Just us, without the rights to lawful assembly,
To be able to freely voice our disagreement with leadership and the stereotypes of society.
Yet when tournament time comes and cars get turned and businesses get looted, no one is concerned
Yet peaceful protest they will condemn and when something jumps off just generalize to all of them.
So you say there's enough blame to share on both sides,
We've still got to live together, so you'd better recognize:

That it's not just about you,
Not about your supposed superiority.
It is not about us trying to take something from you; that you feel such a need,
A need to carry torches and wave Confederate flags representing your hatred and greed.

Just I
Just you
Just he, Just she
Just we
Just you
Just they
Just be
Just me
Just you
Just him, just her
Just us
Just you
Just them

When you single just us
Where you single just us
Why you single just us
How you single just us

Just us is not equal to justice
Just us is not equal to justice
Just us does not equal justice
Just us does not equal justice

Just us
No justice
Just us
No justice
Just us
No justice

Closing Remarks and Benediction

We relayed this message not out of anger,
We relayed this message not out of fear,
We relayed this message to shine a light of truth
on a common pain,
A pain, people of color too often feel.

We relayed this message out of a sense of urgency,
The sense that something yet must be said.
An urgency that cries and pleas for justice,
Who will speak for the dead?

We protest and march peacefully in the streets,
Yet our pain is easily dismissed,
Victims become victimized, blamed for the
problems in our community's midst.

We relayed the message of repentance and
redemption,
For there is yet hope for the diseased to be healed
of this racist condition.
We relayed this message with more questions
than answers,
Yet resolve in hearts that the work of love, peace,
and hope are worth striving for.

We relayed this message to put a thought in your
mind,
To trigger a desire to engage to make a mark in
your day and time.
We relayed this message to ignite a flame, a fire
that will not be put out,

That it will burn so deeply within you, your inner activist can't help but shout.

We have spoken these words in tribute and on behalf of brothers and sisters who have gone before,
We must not let their deaths be in vain; silent no more.
We have spoken these words to bring forth details you may have missed in the news,
To create an opportunity for dialogue and through the mountains of adversity tunnel through.

So let me close with the words of benedictive grace:
May the peace of God our Father that passeth all understanding,
Grant you strength to endure, faith to move mountains, and courage to stand.
May the peace of God comfort your heart when it's heavy with grief,
May you find rest in Him for your weary soul and your mind embraced in His peace.
May the grace, peace, joy, love of God cover you all now, henceforth and evermore.

Printed and bound by PG in the USA